GRAPHIC DESIGN FOR
ARCHITECTS

A MANUAL FOR VISUAL COMMUNICATION

WRITTEN AND DESIGNED BY

KAREN LEWIS

First published 2015
by Routledge
2 Park Square, Milton Park, Abingdon, Oxon OX14 4RN

Simultaneously published in the USA and Canada
by Routledge
711 Third Avenue, New York, NY 10017

Routledge is an imprint of the Taylor & Francis Group, an informa business

British Library Cataloguing in Publication Data
A catalogue record for this book is available from the British Library

Library of Congress Cataloging in Publication Data
Lewis, Karen (Karen Jane)
Graphic design for architects : a manual for visual communication / Karen Lewis.
pages cm
Includes bibliographical references and index.
1. Graphic arts—Handbooks, manuals, etc. 2. Visual communication—Handbooks, manuals, etc.
3. Communication in architecture. I. Title.
NC997.L485 2015
741.602'472—dc23
2014033670

ISBN: 978-0-415-52260-1 (hbk)
ISBN: 978-0-415-52261-8 (pbk)
ISBN: 978-1-315-73156-8 (ebk)

Typeset in Gotham Narrow
by Hoefler & Frere-Jones

Univers and News Gothic
by Linotype

Publisher's Note:
This book has been prepared from camera-ready copy provided by the author.

Printed by Bell & Bain Ltd, Glasgow.

GRAPHIC DESIGN FOR
ARCHITECTS

A MANUAL FOR VISUAL COMMUNICATION

WRITTEN AND DESIGNED BY

KAREN LEWIS

Routledge
Taylor & Francis Group

LONDON AND NEW YORK

THANK YOU

ACKNOWLEDGEMENTS

This book would not be possible without inspiration, creativity and support from many people.

INTERVIEWS

Many thanks to those who were interviewed for this book. Your insights and imagination have enriched this project tremendously.

Tobias Armborst
Luke Bulman
Daniel D'Oca
Nicholas Felton
Anne Filson
Janette Kim
Prem Krishnamurthy
William O'Brien Jr.
Michael Piper
Michael Rock
Scott Stowell
Georgeen Theodore
Benjamin Van Dyke

CONTRIBUTORS

Thank you for the beautiful examples provided by:

Kristy Balliet
Matthew Banton
Nicholas Castillo
Brandon Clifford
Aaron Frazier
Brian Haulter
Elijah Huge
Brian Koehler
Lisl Kotheimer
Kayle Langford
Michael Odum
Michael Piper
Frank Ruchala
Matthew Storrie
Jessie Wilcox

ILLUSTRATIONS

Many thanks to the following students for their image skills:

Ben Flaute
Brian Koehler
Scott McLemore
Michael Odum
Cheyenne Vandervoorde

Many of my own projects in this book involved the intellectual and creative talents of my students, as well as those of **Matthew Banton**, **Sean Burkholder** and **Jason Kentner**.

EDITORIAL

Thanks to the entire **Routledge/Taylor & Francis** team. **Fran Ford**'s unflappable enthusiasm and for first seeing the potential of this project. **Laura Williamson** for her thoughtful guidance, **Emma Gadsden** for her focus and **Grace Harrison** for her encouragement in seeing it through until the end.

Special thanks to the thoughtful **Tomas Campe** for his keen typographic attention.

INSTITUTIONS

The Knowlton School of Architecture at Ohio State University has provided academic and financial support to explore this book's themes and trajectories. I'm grateful to my colleagues for their curiosity and interest. Many thanks to directors **Ann Pendleton-Julian** and **Michael Cadwell** for their support and encouragement; **Beth Blostein** and **Jane Amidon** for their insights and enthusiasm. Many thanks to **Jeffrey Kipnis** for his deep attention and thoughtful comments.

Many thanks to **University of Kentucky** for their support. **David Biagi**, **David Mohney** and **Michael Speaks** supported this project in its earliest development.

COMMUNITIES

Before I interned at the **National Building Museum** and the **Bruce Museum**, I was introduced to exhibition design during a lecture at **Wellesley College**. I'm proud to be part of an institution that opens minds as well as hearts.

Icon Nicholson changed the way I work as a designer. I'm forever grateful for the people I met there, especially for **Alex Tween**.

Developing my thesis at the **Harvard University Graduate School of Design** opened worlds I'm still uncovering. A lifetime of thanks to **Sarah Whiting** and **Ron Witte** for their support and mutual curiosity, and to **John Stilgoe** for his deep and inspired attention.

PEOPLE

This book first began over crackers and conversations with the incandescently brilliant **Wallis Miller**.

For 15 years, **Julia McMorrough** has been an inspiration and model for what being an architect can be.

John McMorrough has provided support, inspiration and guidance at every stage. He is a steadfast teacher, mentor, critic and friend.

All of my work is better when **Matthew Banton** is involved.

Jason Kentner, my dearest friend and design partner. You guard my dreams and visions.

This project is dedicated to my family—**Mom**, **Dad**, **Woo**. All roads are easier with you.

TABLE OF CONTENTS

ARCHITECTS FOR GRAPHIC DESIGN

KAREN LEWIS

Architects describe their work through drawings, images and models. Increasingly, architects use other forms of representation to describe their ideas. Diagrams, information graphics, books, posters, websites, competition boards and digital presentations are part of an expanded vocabulary of representation techniques. While the topic of these drawings is architecture, the tools and techniques used to present them are expertise associated with graphic design. Deep disciplinary knowledge is required to produce architecture; however, additional knowledge from graphic design is necessary to present architecture.

More and more architects are responsible for images that explain the effects of architecture, be they financial, organizational, environmental or social. As the architecture profession becomes more specialized, workflow increasingly complex and design expertise further focused, architects are required to produce a wider range of drawings to explain the impacts of their work. It is common for architects to produce a broad range of representations to communicate with clients, project consultants or public constituencies. The architect's graphic output is no longer limited to two-dimensional representations of three-dimensional space, but also includes drawings of organization, structure and relationships across building materials, finance and other consultancies. These images, prepared by the architect as part of the design process, represent the organization of interrelated decisions.

As architecture expands its reach of visual services, these methods of structuring and organizing space move beyond that of client-designer relationships. The way work is presented

graphically communicates design's conceptual and intellectual framework. For example, in the MoMA PS1 Young Architects Program, design teams produce a range of representations to explain their proposal. Traditional orthographic drawings have been augmented—if not entirely replaced—by renderings, diagrams and animations. Work is not pinned on the wall cohesively but presented via slide-by-slide presentations of single images and videos. Recently, too, design teams prepare project books for each juror. The intellectual shift away from traditional drawings towards an expanded vocabularly of representations that include presentations, diagrams, renderings and books— further two-dimensional representations of an architectural project—has become part of an architect's spatial strategies. These expanded representation techniques are foundational to how an architectural proposal is imagined. The graphic presentation of architecture is not an additional lens of expertise applied to the presentation of work; it is essential to the way architecture is conceived, developed and projected. Graphics are not about the addition of further, unaffiliated expertise layered upon those of architecture—to do so is an anathema—but it is to recognize the relationship between representation and the work itself. Contemporary representation techniques are imbued within architecture's spatial and organizational techniques. These comprise the same lineage of spatial structures that guide and shape its development.

Architects—indeed, all professions—need to understand the foundations of graphic design in order to present articulately information. Visual communication is an increasingly significant part of professional communication. Architects in particular can benefit from this knowledge to enhance representation skills, but also to facilitate better relationships with consultants. Every building, landscape or urban center eventually interacts with graphic designers. Having knowledge of graphic design's potential can better position architects to communicate and collaborate with their consultants. In the same way architects have engaged affiliated professions such as structural engineering and landscape architecture, architects can and should foster similar creative collaborations with graphic designers. Instead of adding graphic designers to the final stages of a building's construction to add signage, for example, graphic designers should be included much earlier in the design process. To do so allows both the architecture and building graphics to share similar conceptual agendas. 2x4 and OMA's collaboration at the Illinois Institute of Technology McCormick Tribune Center rested upon a shared intellectual query surrounding perception. Koolhaas's essay "Junk Space" was first published in *ANY 27*, which 2x4 designed. This shared question of visual perception stimulated the building's graphic treatment. Walls host information, using graphic design as a way to both encode and obfuscate the surface. At the McCormick Center the building's graphics are part of a shared spatial project between the graphic designer and architect.

Conversely, architecture without graphic design can produce unintended spatial effects. Scoggin and Elam's Knowlton School of Architecture at Ohio State University is a building with clear spatial hierarchies. However, its unconventional use of ramps, walls and materials makes navigation confounding for a user accustomed to the spatial strategies of traditional campus buildings. Users entering the building looking for the main auditorium, Room 250, immediately search for access to the second floor. Ignoring the spatial cues provided by main volumes and wide ramps directing users to prominent spaces, the unfamiliar visitor immediately proceeds up small, narrow staircases to arrive at the second floor. At the beginning of every semester ad hoc signage litters the building walls, attempting to direct visitors towards the main thoroughfares. These signs are unproductive. Printed (or hand-drawn) on single sheets of white letter-sized paper, the small rectangles disappear within the grey, concrete, 20-foot entry spaces. Located haphazardly, the signs fall out of the user's view. As such, these graphic messages do not correlate to the building's space.

Architects do not need to become graphic designers; we need to understand better the expertise and techniques of graphic design. Expanding our graphic representation skills allows communication with broader audiences, clients, and research collaborators and facilitates disciplinary knowledge across related fields. Architecture also needs to recognize the spatial practice shared with graphic design. A closer relationship between the two disciplines will enhance the intelligence of both fields. Understanding how architecture is visually spatial, how graphic designers design space, and how the two disciplines can imbue the other with further intelligence can only increase each discipline's spatial knowledge. Architects are not trained as graphic designers and its important for the discipline to recognize its limitations. But increasing our awareness of graphic design techniques will allow architects to share questions about space, navigation, surface and perception with graphic designers. To include graphic design and graphic designers within our discipline expands opportunities for spatial invention.

2X4

MICHAEL ROCK, CREATIVE DIRECTOR / NEW YORK, NY

1

MICHAEL ROCK *is a founding partner and Creative Director at 2x4 and Director of the Graphic Architecture Project at the Columbia University Graduate School of Architecture, Planning and Preservation. At 2x4, he leads a wide range of projects for Prada, Nike, Kanye West, Barneys New York, Harvard and CCTV. His writing on design has appeared in publications worldwide. He is the recipient of the 1999/2000 Rome Prize in Design from the American Academy in Rome.*

GRAPHIC DESIGN FOR ARCHITECTS: You've been crafting the Graphic Architecture Project at the Graduate School of Architecture at Columbia University. What is the relationship between graphic design and architecture?

MICHAEL ROCK: I don't think so much about graphic design benefiting architecture; more often I think that architecture is often a form of graphic design. A significant percentage of the work of architecture is two-dimensional representation—drawings, renderings, diagrams, collages—and texts. It's basically the ingredients in graphic

design. In school, with the exception of model-making, students' work is almost exclusively graphic. Critiques are centered in presentations in the form of boards and Power Point presentations. Very little of the work actually becomes built form but there is hardly any discussion about the material quality of that work.

I started the Graphic Architecture Project with the statement: architecture is born of, and dies as, graphic design. As almost all the work before a building is built is graphic, the building lives on in the form of media coverage, photographs, essays, etc. We only visit a miniscule percentage of the world's buildings; the rest we know through

2 3

pictures, blogs, books, articles. Your understanding of architecture is primarily through the graphic, not the spatial.

GDA: Graphic design programs teach typography, layout, color theory. Those topics aren't typically covered in a traditional architecture representation course. From a curricular standpoint, how is architecture graphic design?

MR: Architects make drawings, renderings, books, diagrams, all as forms of persuasion. The subject is architecture, but the form of it is graphic. In a way the subject isn't that important. It's the composition of

graphic material to create a certain effect, assembling images on pages to a specific end—to evoke a design, a building or a concept. Manipulating two-dimensional objects on paper, on screens and in space is the operation of graphic design.

GDA: What is the subject of the Graphic Architecture Project?

MR: GAP focuses on all of the graphic issues in, on, around and about architecture. We look at presentation and how ideas are broadcast, how content is injected in space, how media interacts with form. I've been working on a series of

classes on the sub-genres of architecture. For example, I've been teaching a class on diagrams. I use Koolhaas's definition: the diagram is the reduction of an idea down to its most fundamental contradiction. The diagram is about juxtaposition. Before you have a building you have a diagram that addresses issues of program, flows, narratives. The diagram is the most primitive representation of the process. We try to look at how the diagram may inform the design process.

We did another class looking at display, the electronic display as a hyper-specialized building material. If the diagram is the earliest act, display is the latest thing, the activation of the surface. What kind of material is a display? Is it a window? Is it a wall? It's a prominent part of many buildings entire facades are given over to it and as a material it's one of the most expensive. But we don't think about it materially. It's a hybrid form.

GDA: You make the point earlier that graphic design doesn't add value to architecture because architecture is graphic design. However, at the scale of a wall in a building, it sounds as if you're saying that graphic design does add value to architecture. Is that true?

MR: In economics, if you buy an egg you get an egg. But if you do something to the egg it's worth more. You've given form to it so now it is a better product than it was before. Graphic design does that, too. You have space and you have walls and graphic design does something to those things that adds value to them. It's the same thing with text. You get raw, underdeveloped text then you shape it, you add value to it, and now the text has the qualities of the book and you've added value onto the text itself. You can think about that in spatial terms, too, that you add design so that it adds value to space.

GDA: How does graphic design operate at the scale of a wall?

MR: The wall is a condition in the way the page is a condition. Walls are facts that you're constantly working against. They are solid, they hold things up, they are opaque. They have a series of qualities that always need to be grappled with. When we started the project at Prada Store in Soho by OMA, the idea of using wallpaper as a major gesture was a very loaded act for a work of a high architect.

Wallpaper is definitely not architectural. It's a low form of decoration that serves no structural or material function. It is utterly superficial. Since wallpaper is not architecture, it must be about something else: class, taste, image, representation and meaning. Wallpaper, it would seem, is an admission of an architectural failure.

We took this idea of superficial very seriously and tried to interrogate what it meant. The very fact the wallpaper is temporary, that it changes every six months or so, creates the condition wherein you're always referring to your own superficiality. And because it's temporal, wallpaper can do a very specific, detailed job. It can be targeted and contextual in a way the building cannot.

The Prada wallpaper took a rhetorical form in that we were always engaging the space itself—the presence, opacity, the fact of the wall—as well as content related to the meaning of the space, that is its about fashion, luxury, Italianness, bourgeois culture, shopping, etc. We're always trying to enhance the breadth of the wall, its thickness, flatness, impenetrability, or we're scheming to make the wall disappear. If you think about those formal challenges—and this is where it ties in specifically to graphic design—the subject of the work is always the problem itself. In this case the wallpaper is only a millimeter thick, it literally has almost no Z-dimension. So depth is always an illusion. It can have perspectival depth, conceptual depth, intellectual depth, but its inherent flatness is the essential formal, graphic problem. Metaphorically, wallpaper is the same as graphic design; we're always trying to impose depth.

GDA: How were you experimenting with depth at the Illinois Institute of Technology (IIT) McCormick Student Center?

MR: At the student center at IIT the walls are just gypsum dividers, the roof is supported by a steel I-beam grid that is disengaged from the walls. Right about the time we were working on the project with OMA, Koolhaas was writing "Junk Space" that ended up in *ANY 27* (2000) which we designed. (Later I told him we were influenced by the essay, and the idea of IIT as a kind of junk space, and he noted he was thinking about Pompeii and some of the deepest, most solid architectural issues.) At IIT we were thinking about the walls as superficial partitions, surfaces onto which we applied coatings to give them meaning. So a fancy wall is a gold wall, a rough room has a sheetrock wall. The walls were signs that coded spaces and the project was a catalogue of graphic devices, all of these different ways to change the meaning of spaces based on appliqué.

The graphic elements of IIT were about always trying effect vision in a new way: far and close, deep and shallow, etc. They are all embedded in the spaces around the student center. The building holds all of the effects that you experience if you approach it from a distance and it engages you as you move through the space. That's a project we've been trying to keep going on our own for a long time.

GDA: How do buildings communicate? Mark Wigley speaks about the relationship between architecture and words in his introduction to *Multiple Signatures*. But you address how images, rather than words, communicate. How do you grapple with communication beyond words?

MR: I've been struggling with that because when communication becomes too blatant, too literal, it becomes a negative value to the building. It is compensatory. For example, the library is shaped like

4

a gigantic book or the concert hall is shaped like a gigantic drum; everything is shaped like its program. Anytime the built form becomes literal I find it diminished. Buildings may, however, become brand devices as a residual part of a communication strategy; they become representative of a corporate or organizational ethos. We're a daring organization, so our architecture should be daring too. The form is a statement of values. It's an unusual thing. Everyone knows about Bilbao because they've seen representations of it. It's even spawned a theory: the so-called Bilbao Effect. Frank Gehry has built a career on the idea that his work immediately represents innovation and confidence.

GDA: How has the design work of branding evolved in your practice?

MR: The idea of branding has drastically transformed in the last 25 years. When I was studying graphic design it was called corporate identity and it involved creating scalable, rational design systems that organized the visual material of an organization or enterprise. The goal was to create a big manual that organized the logo, typeface, color system and the way those things would be displayed. This was design based in uniformity and rules. There are lots of designers who have done that very successfully for a very long time. (You could argue that both Imperial Rome and the Han Dynasty created very specific rules about representation and broadcast those

rules across their vast empires.) Over the past few decades there has been a move away from uniformity of visualization and toward a uniformity of voice. Designers started to come to the conclusion that the goal of branding was the construction of a consistent personality, strong enough to be modulated for different audiences. At the same time, branding was picked up as a major case study in business schools and business journalists started to report on it. In the course of my career we have moved from a condition in which no one had any idea what design was, to it becoming a ubiquitous subject. Now everyone is using branding as a lens through which everything is practiced. Every entity from nations and global alliances down to local schools and individuals are obsessed with

reputation and voice are more valuable than all of its real estate, buildings, trucks, bottle, ingredients, everything. So what are these things that make your brand? A brand is both an ideology and a planning tool. A brand vision provides a way to evaluate how to move forward, to grow and change. If you're a city, and you're trying to figure out how to develop, a brand gives you a sense of how to organize zoning and program. It makes you aware of who you are and what you're about so that it helps you make planning decisions. Branding is about the future of things you're going to do rather than what you're doing now. It's about what you're going to do next.

It's interesting to think about Austin, Texas, which has a very specific feel to it. Its slogan is "Keep Austin Weird." That says to me it's a city that really knows what is valuable about itself. And that means you make very specific types of decisions in urban planning, transportation, everything. If you're keeping that identity in mind it's going to tell you about how people are going to live, move, zone your city. It's a system about making design choices.

On the practical side we've seen big changes in our own projects. It used to be that we started with a logo and some colors. Now those things come very late to the process. Almost all of our work now is about finding the core messages of an organization and understanding where it's going. How do they speak? What can they say, credibly? Then we design stuff that supports that position. Logos are the third stage of the project. It's very rare for us to work with someone who says "I need a logo." Now it's about defining the organization's personality.

GDA: What are the processes you use to develop that type of abstract conversation?

MR: We spend a lot of time interviewing and talking to people, and just trying to understand ourselves. But mostly it's about creativity and imagination. It's like we are creating a personality. We try to describe our clients' companies the way you would tell me about someone you knew and I didn't. You'd resort to a handful of adjectives. What about a museum? You can do the same thing. You can say it's an open place, it's totally unpretentious, it's dynamic, or grand, or intimate. What kind of place it is? It's the most refined, elegant place you've ever been, Don't go with your kids, *ever*. If you start to describe an organization in the same way then it starts to give you a feeling of how you should design for them, not just their

7

stuff but their practices too. Because now you're designing a person more than you're designing this abstract thing.

GDA: It is hard for institutions to think about their identities as having multiple voices, different forms of execution.

MR: The hardest part is the internal part. How do you get your workforce to think the same way? Oftentimes when people come to us, their staff is unclear about what they should be doing. The first stage is always the internal phase—how does the idea of this institution affect the way you do your work in this institution? We've been working recently with a huge botanical garden and we were talking about this place as a heterotopia, a totally different world that mirrors but is set apart from the real one. So, you then ask the

person working at the gatehouse. "If this place is a world apart, how would you do your job differently?" Maybe you shouldn't have a gate. Maybe you walk up and have a more natural exchange. You start to think about the ways you do all of these jobs differently. Working from these kinds of platforms, people tend to act differently. There are brands that do that really well. Apple, for example. The Apple Store has little to do with how the store looks. They train their staff really well. People act towards you in a certain way that makes you feel this is a special place.

GDA: Is branding architecture?

MR: That's a really good question. I would have to think back as to what architecture is. What do you think architecture is?

GDA: I think architecture is about how we live, the design of systems, conditions and spaces that structure our lives.

MR: Well, then, branding is a form of architecture because it's structuring a social engagement. Architecture structures social engagements in lots of different ways and to that end, branding is the same thing because it gives meaning to how we live.

↑ **GRAPHIC PROJECTS**

1: Prada Store, New York, NY

2–6: Illinois Institute of Technology (IIT) McCormick Student Center, Chicago, IL

7: Nike 100 Exhibition

PRESENTING YOURSELF

PORTFOLIOS

GETTING STARTED

PORTFOLIOS CAN TAKE MANY FORMS. Knowing which form will work best for your needs can be a complex set of questions—is this portfolio for getting a job or graduate school? How will you produce your portfolio? Will the work be reviewed digitally or physically? And how many pages should your portfolio include?

Context influences Curation   *Production and Form are related*

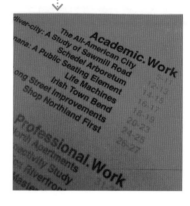

1 CONTEXT

WHAT'S THE PORTFOLIO FOR?
Context can influence the final form your portfolio will take. Consider one of the typical portfolio scenarios:

Graduate schools are interested in your ideas so begin with work that shows who you are as a designer. Use your portfolio to show how you think visually.

Employers want to see your school work *and* your professional accomplishments. If you don't have any office experience, demonstrate your professionalism through a neat and organized portfolio.

Academic appointments need to show your research, teaching and service efforts. Make sure to emphasize your research and to separate clearly student work from your own design projects.

2 PRODUCTION

WHY START WITH THIS?
How you'll design, print and bind or output your work puts useful technical constraints on your portfolio design.

QUESTIONS TO ASK
How will you print your portfolio?
Knowing this up front will establish all other design decisions.

What is your budget? Number of pages, full bleeds and portfolio size can impact cost.

What resources are available? Will you order your supplies online or do you want to be able to run to the office supply store if you run out of paper? Knowing your own work habits can help make decisions. If you want to work to the last minute, you may not want to rely on sending your portfolio to be printed online.

3 CURATION

WHAT WORK TO SHOW?
Include projects that demonstrate your ability to think visually and spatially—studio, art, graphics and other artistic work are good choices, especially if your background in architecture is limited.

THINGS TO CONSIDER
How many pages long should each project be? Depends on the work. More important than number of pages is clarity and organization. A single, well-composed page is preferable to many cluttered pages.

What if you don't have any architecture background at all? The portfolio shows how you think visually, so don't shy away from examples from other fields. Paintings from art seminars, diagrams from sports performances or even biology lab observation reports can be excellent examples.

Many architects think portfolio design is just this phase

Lots of back and forth   *Lots of back and forth*

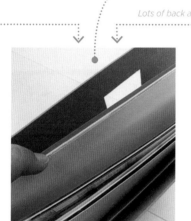

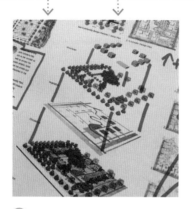

④ FORM

WHAT SHOULD IT LOOK LIKE?
A better question to ask is "What should it look like?" Bright and white? Rigid and substantial? Soft and flexible? How will the context—graduate school, a professional job, a teaching position—set up conditions for the portfolio's atmosphere?

THINGS TO CONSIDER
Landscape versus portrait? When opened, landscape-oriented portfolios become super landscapes, which can be hard to design. Portrait-oriented pages have the potential for landscape and portrait images.

Think about organization rather than "graphic design," as the guiding effort for your portfolio. This will help you from over-designing your portfolio.

⑤ EDITING

WHAT IS THIS PHASE?
Editing is more than spell-check—it's printing the portfolio out and looking at it as a physical thing. During the editing process you can see how photos could change in size, how text should better scale to the page and what parts of the projects can be edited to make your work clear.

THINGS TO PREPARE FOR
Work on the screen looks really different than when it is printed. Typefaces look gigantic and colors print darker. Do a few test prints well before your final design phase to make these needed adjustments.

Crop your pages before you make scale decisions. Seeing extra white space around a small portfolio printed on a regular sheet of paper can influence your perception.

⑥ IMPLEMENTATION

THINGS TO KEEP IN MIND
Whether preparing your files to hand to the printer, or getting your pages back and deciding to crop them, the final process of implementing your design is exciting.

THINGS TO CONSIDER
Take your time putting your portfolio together. It can take longer than you think. Build in extra time to your process to output, prepare and organize your work.

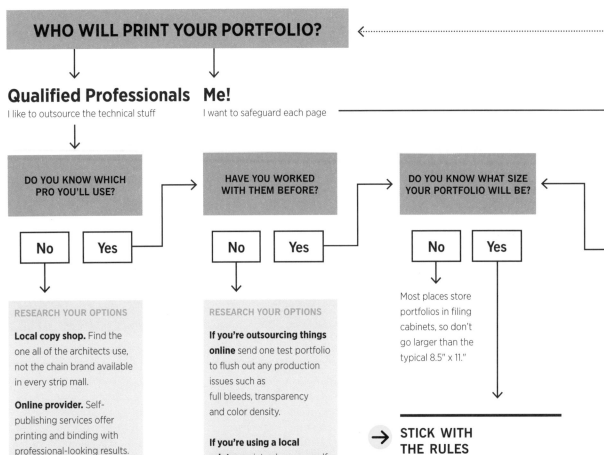

WHO WILL PRINT YOUR PORTFOLIO?

Qualified Professionals
I like to outsource the technical stuff

Me!
I want to safeguard each page

DO YOU KNOW WHICH PRO YOU'LL USE?

No   Yes

HAVE YOU WORKED WITH THEM BEFORE?

No   Yes

DO YOU KNOW WHAT SIZE YOUR PORTFOLIO WILL BE?

No   Yes

RESEARCH YOUR OPTIONS

Local copy shop. Find the one all of the architects use, not the chain brand available in every strip mall.

Online provider. Self-publishing services offer printing and binding with professional-looking results. But be careful—student projects can appear under developed a monograph print. Ironically, too, some providers are known for inconsistent printing quality.

RESEARCH YOUR OPTIONS

If you're outsourcing things online send one test portfolio to flush out any production issues such as full bleeds, transparency and color density.

If you're using a local printer go introduce yourself. Meet the staff and explain your project. They can offer advice on file preparation, suggest paper and binding techniques, and help make the process run more smoothly.

Files that aren't set up properly are one of the most frequent complaints from printers. If your portfolio has full-bleed images, make sure to set up your file with full bleeds.

Most places store portfolios in filing cabinets, so don't go larger than the typical 8.5" x 11."

→ **STICK WITH THE RULES**

Are you applying to graduate school or for a fellowship or internship? If they've made restrictions or specifications for your application size, **follow these specifications exactly**. You don't want to annoy anyone before you've even been accepted!

List any known portfolio limits here:

Portfolio thickness ....
# of projects ....
# of pages ....
Name on each page? ....
On the cover? ....
Anything else? ....

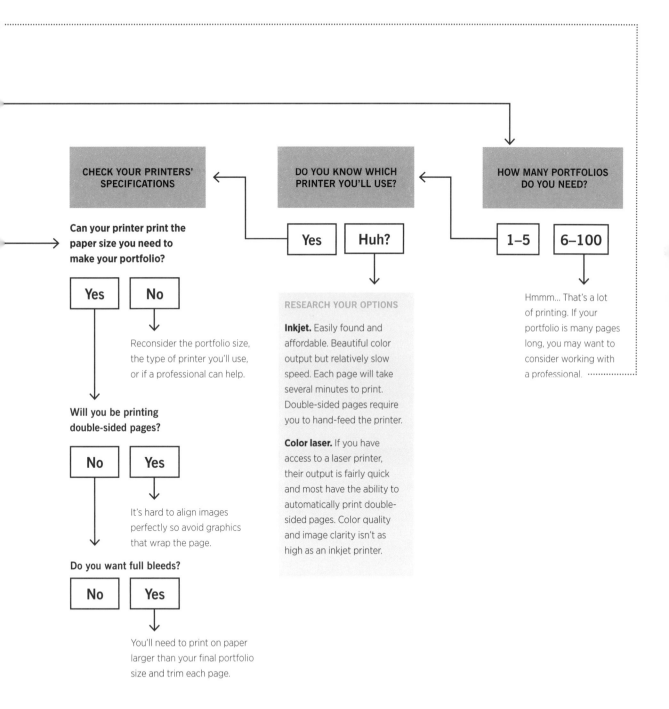

CHECK YOUR PRINTERS' SPECIFICATIONS

Can your printer print the paper size you need to make your portfolio?

Yes | No

No → Reconsider the portfolio size, the type of printer you'll use, or if a professional can help.

Will you be printing double-sided pages?

No | Yes

Yes → It's hard to align images perfectly so avoid graphics that wrap the page.

Do you want full bleeds?

No | Yes

Yes → You'll need to print on paper larger than your final portfolio size and trim each page.

DO YOU KNOW WHICH PRINTER YOU'LL USE?

Yes | Huh?

Huh? →

RESEARCH YOUR OPTIONS

Inkjet. Easily found and affordable. Beautiful color output but relatively slow speed. Each page will take several minutes to print. Double-sided pages require you to hand-feed the printer.

Color laser. If you have access to a laser printer, their output is fairly quick and most have the ability to automatically print double-sided pages. Color quality and image clarity isn't as high as an inkjet printer.

HOW MANY PORTFOLIOS DO YOU NEED?

1–5 | 6–100

6–100 → Hmmm... That's a lot of printing. If your portfolio is many pages long, you may want to consider working with a professional.

PRODUCING YOUR PORTFOLIO

THE WAY YOUR PORTFOLIO WILL BE PRODUCED—printed and bound or presented digitally—can put useful constraints on how you'll design your portfolio. Thinking of what technologies you'll use to produce the portfolio will help guide many other design decisions.

DIGITAL PORTFOLIOS

Submitting your portfolio to one graduate school as a physical submission, and to another as a digital file, can make things hectic. Streamline your efforts by considering a few things.

SPREADS TO SCREEN
In portrait orientation, output your page spreads to fit on the screen.

portrait   portrait   screen

PAGE TO SCREEN
In landscape orientation, output single pages to fit on the screen.

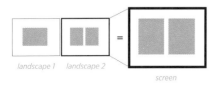

landscape 1   landscape 2   screen

BREAK INTO SCREENS
Break apart a presentation into linear, singular screen images.

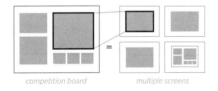

competition board   multiple screens

PRINTING IT YOURSELF

Do you want to work to the last minute? Try as we might, we often need every minute of time to get the design right. If you know you'll need to work to the last minute, you'll want to invest in your own inkjet printer and print the pages yourself.

USEFUL HINTS
- Try to use readily available resources.
- If you're committed to ordering special paper, order three times what you think you'll need.
- Test a few pages on different settings. Each page can take up to three minutes to print, so account for printing time when designing portfolio production.

↓ CROP IT OUT

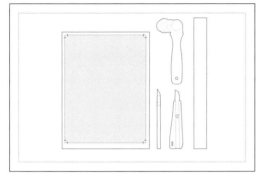

1 GATHER TOOLS

You will need the following:

- **Cutting mat**
- **Straight-edge ruler (preferably with cork backing)**
- **Knife or another type of hand-held paper trimmer.**

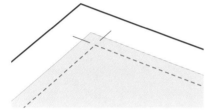

2 CROP MARKS

These should be inset into the page bleed. Make sure you've printed your portfolio with crop marks and bleed settings turned on.

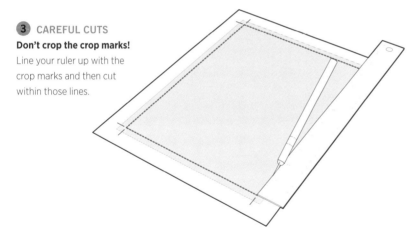

3 CAREFUL CUTS

Don't crop the crop marks!
Line your ruler up with the crop marks and then cut within those lines.

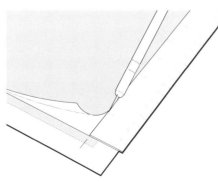

4 FINISHED PAGE

Your final portfolio page will pop out from the cut paper leaving behind a "window frame" with the bleed margins and crop marks remaining.

NOTES ON:

FULL BLEEDS

In order to guarantee a full bleed, set the portfolio file with a minimum of 3–6mm bleeds. This bleed margin gives printers flexibility in case trimming and crop marks don't line up precisely. With a bleed there's extra image to hide any slight misalignment that might occur between the page edge and crop.

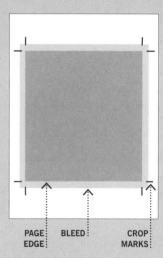

| PAGE EDGE | BLEED | CROP MARKS |

Because the image will extend beyond the edge of the page, you'll need to print on paper that is larger than your portfolio size. Printers charge by the size of paper they need to print on, not the final size.

Portfolio Size	Paper Size
8.5" x 11"	11" x 14"
8" x 10.5"	8.5" x 11"
8.5" x 8.5"	11" x 14"
8" x 8"	8.5" x 11"

 ↑ **Slightly changing portfolio size can make a difference in printing costs.**

23

BINDING OPTIONS

BINDING PLAYS A BIG PART IN THE OVERALL DESIGN and construction of the portfolio. Binding contributes to the atmopshere of your portfolio. It should be quiet, as unobtrusive as possible and, of course, facilitate your ability to open the portfolio. Will the book lay flat? Will the images be continuous? How you approach these questions will have an impact on the binding.

When opened, coil-bound books will lay flat on a surface

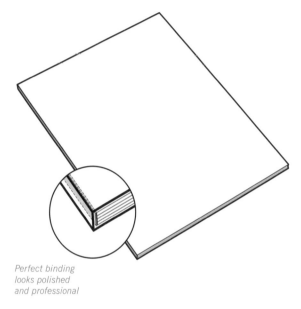

Perfect binding looks polished and professional

 METAL O-RING BINDING

WHY IT'S GREAT

- An easy and inexpensive binding option
- Book lays flat when open (a big bonus!)

LOOK OUT FOR

Plastic coil binding. Never use plastic. It looks and feels cheap and can snag the paper.

Metal O-ring coils can be difficult to locate. Consider purchasing your own binding machine if you're committed to this method and cannot find a professional resource.

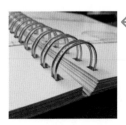

← **Coil scale** can make a big difference in portfolio presentation. If your book is small and thick, the large coil needed to hold many pages can look too large.

 PERFECT BINDING

WHY IT'S GREAT

- Clean and neat; looks like a professional book
- Images seamlessly span the book spine

LOOK OUT FOR

Looking too professional. If the book looks too much like a professional monograph, the reader expects professional-looking work. Student projects might look out of place in this context.

Finding a local printing service that offers perfect binding can be difficult. Most do not offer this binding option. If you're committed to a perfect bind, you'll likely have to print and bind through an online provider. Online providers' page print qualities can be inconsistent so give yourself plenty of time for quality checks.

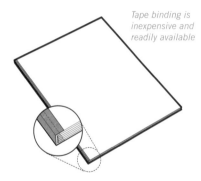

Tape binding is inexpensive and readily available

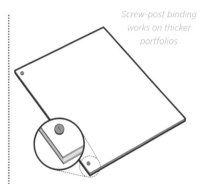

Screw-post binding works on thicker portfolios

↑ TAPE BINDING

WHY IT'S GREAT

- Inexpensive and readily available alternative to perfect binding

LOOK OUT FOR

Portfolio thickness. Tape binding works for books less than 1/2" thick. Tape colors are usually limited to white or black (although someone once "clad" her tape bind with hot orange tape!)

Cover. Unless you're going to cover the book with a jacket or sleeve, incorporate the tape edge as part of the cover design.

↑ SCREW-POST BINDING

WHY IT'S GREAT

- Works well for portfolios that are too thick for tape binding.
- With the proliferation of scrap booking, materials are easy to find

LOOK OUT FOR

Opening the book. If you're using heavier, stiffer paper, this binding method can make your book difficult to open

Cover. Use a cover to mask the presence of the posts. Overly techtonic portfolios are very "early 90s decon."

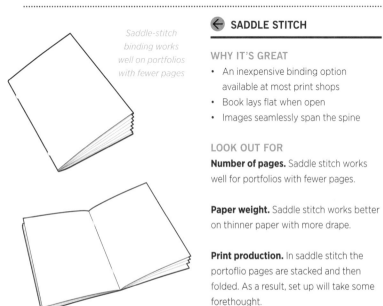

Saddle-stitch binding works well on portfolios with fewer pages

← SADDLE STITCH

WHY IT'S GREAT

- An inexpensive binding option available at most print shops
- Book lays flat when open
- Images seamlessly span the spine

LOOK OUT FOR

Number of pages. Saddle stitch works well for portfolios with fewer pages.

Paper weight. Saddle stitch works better on thinner paper with more drape.

Print production. In saddle stitch the portoflio pages are stacked and then folded. As a result, set up will take some forethought.

NOTES ON:

BINDINGS TO AVOID

There are a few binding types that can detract from your portfolio presentation.

ANYTHING PLASTIC

The portfolio is a tactile experience, not just a visual one. Plastic coils, plastic sleeves and covers can make your work feel, and subsequently appear, cheap and flimsy.

OFF-THE-SHELF FOLIOS

Most art stores sell two types of folios: inexpensive, black plastic folders, or expensive, metal binders. Neither of these are good options as they can make your work look unfinished. The plastic folios can make your work look flimsy and cheap, and the metal binders can be too stiff and shiny.

CRAFTY BINDING

If done with precision, hand-sewn bindings can be subtle and sensitive. However, they take a lot of time and can quickly become overly precious. Be cautious.

ARTICULATED BINDING

Never use anything that hyper-articulates the book's techtonics such as nuts, bolts, twigs, ribbons, wire, twine... Don't confuse a serious presentation of your work with the chance to "express yourself." The portfolio is not a scrap book.

25

COVER OPTIONS

THE COVER IS AN EXTENSION OF YOUR PORTFOLIO INTERIOR. Until you design your portfolio pages, you cannot really design what the cover will look like graphically. However, you can and should be thinking about the tactile experience of your portfolio and what materials will help support this intention. Will your cover be hard or soft? Sturdy or delicate? Thinking through these physical options will help you make other decisions.

The hand-made jacket is a durable, elegant sleeve for the wire-bound portfolio that slides into the back flap

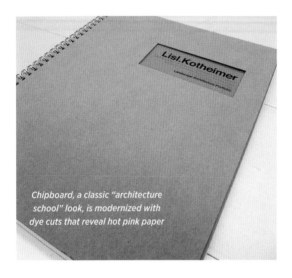

Chipboard, a classic "architecture school" look, is modernized with dye cuts that reveal hot pink paper

 HARD COVERS

WHY THEY ARE GREAT
Durable and strong, hard covers will protect the sheets within and withstand multiple pairs of hands looking at the work.

MATERIALS
Rigid materials that have no flexibility or bend, such as **chipboard, museum board, plastic or book board**.

BINDING OPTIONS
Due to their lack of flexibility, hard covers work well with binding that offers no resistance, such as **coil binding**.

LOOK OUT FOR
Gratuitous laser cutting. Just because you have the technology doesn't mean you should use it. Cutting perforations through transparent plexiglass is hardly effective, and no one likes burnt chipboard. Think carefully and critically before using the laser cutter to design your portfolio cover.

Traditional book-binding techniques. There are ways other than metal O-ring to bind hard covers, but getting too crafty with your portfolio can send the wrong message—suddenly you have a scrap book! Or it looks like you're trying too hard to "design" the binding. If done with precision and executed perfectly, hand sewing can be subtle and beautiful, albeit labor intensive. Proceed with caution.

ADDITIONAL DESIGN COMPONENTS
- **Dye cuts** can be used to add openings. Talk with your printer / binder about dyes already available.

- **Customize your portfolio** by adding a printed half-sheet of paper bound to the coils.

- **Foil printing, stamping, or embossing** your cover are other ways to add visual interest.

A NOTE ABOUT COVER DESIGN

Keep it super simple. A plain cover or simple graphic element with your name is sufficient. Using photos or graphic trends will quickly become outdated; also, stay away from putting the date on the cover, too. The minute the year changes, your portfolio is instantly outdated.

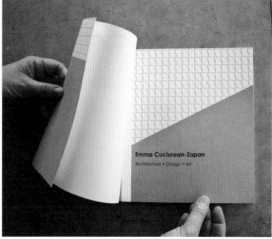

 SOFT COVERS

WHY THEY ARE GREAT

They make your portfolio feel more like an actual book— professionally published and available in a bookstore. Finishing options are more varied (matte, glossy) and there is greater flexibility in design.

MATERIALS

Thin, durable materials work best, such as **Bristol paper, card stock, or any heavy weight paper**.

BINDING OPTIONS

Because they are flexible, soft covers work well with many binding types such as **perfect binding, tape binding, and coil binding**.

LOOK OUT FOR

Fragile materials. Thin, flexible materials are likely to tear, especially on coil binding. Overuse can also wear printed paper, revealing snags and tears after a short time.

Vellum. If treated thoughtfully, vellum can be a simple and elegant drape of translucency. If merely added as an extra design element, it can look dated. If not used properly, it's a material that skews into late-90s-deconstruction territory.

ADDITIONAL DESIGN COMPONENTS

Card stock and other materials can be used to divide sections of your portfolio and add thickness to the portfolio form. Due to its super-saturated colored card stock, unlike vellum, is more akin to pantone swatches, illustrator samples and brighter colors that are more contemporary.

Add a belly band or book jacket to a tape- or perfect-bound portfolio to give layer of information, or to hide a seam.

ORGANIZING YOUR WORK

WHAT SORTS OF PROJECTS SHOULD YOU INCLUDE IN YOUR PORTFOLIO?
As always, it depends upon the context. Graduate school? Focus on your school projects, creative work and any professional practice experience you might have. Job in a firm? Highlight your past work experience. Don't have any architecture experience? Other creative work such as drawings or photographs can demonstrate your visual skills.

 FOR GRADUATE SCHOOL

Your list of what to include in your portfolio will change depending on your education and professional background. Students with five-year professional degrees will have very different portfolios from students with an undergraduate double major in, for example, art and math.

FIVE-YEAR PROFESSIONAL DEGREE
With a professional degree your application to graduate school will include more projects that are well developed. It is also expected that candidates will have put their undergraduate degree to use and apply to graduate school after working.

Studio projects
- 5th year fall studio
- 4th year spring travel studio
- 4th year fall urban design studio
- 3rd year fall factory studio
- 3rd year spring housing studio
- 5th year independent study

Other design work
- Travel sketches
- Drawings
- Graphic design projects

Professional work
- Airport competition
- Music hall renovation
- Private house for a client

Writing samples
- Essay from 4th year seminar
- Essay from 5th year history lecture

FOUR-YEAR DEGREE IN ARCHITECTURE, LANDSCAPE OR URBAN DESIGN
Supplement studio projects with design work from seminars, classes and extra curricular experiences.

Architecture
- 3rd year spring studio
- 4th year urban studio
- 3rd year fall studio
- 3rd year winter studio

Fabricated works
- 2nd year spring installation
- Fall furniture seminar

FOUR-YEAR DEGREE IN SOMETHING ELSE ENTIRELY DIFFERENT
Majored in art, women's studies or astronomy? Think creatively about how to demonstrate your ability to abstract and think visually.

- Microscope observations from biology classes
- Maps of Starbucks locations from a seminar on gentrification

Art courses
- Life drawing class
- Photography class
- Intermediate drawing

FOR AN ACADEMIC POSITION

When applying for teaching positions, it's important to emphasize three things: research, teaching and service. Service can be communicated through your CV, but research and teaching should be explained visually in the portfolio. Make sure to demarcate clearly what is your work versus your students' work.

Statements and CV
- CV
- Teaching and Research Statements

Research / design work
- Masters thesis project
- Design projects (such as competitions and other research work) completed outside of school
- Relevant graduate school studio work and coursework that positions your research agenda
- Professional work experience

Teaching examples
- Studios—especially those that highlight your research efforts
- Seminars and independent studies that explore your research topics
- Large lecture courses or other primary coursework that demonstrates how you can contribute to the curriculum

 FOR A JOB

When applying for a job, it's important to demonstrate your disciplinary skills. However, don't limit this to just including construction drawings—firms want to see how you think, too, so emphasize process and design ideas in conjunction with your technical abilities.

Resume and references
- Resume that clearly shows the chronology of your work history
- Names and contact information for references who have already agreed to serve as a reference

Academic work
- Masters thesis project
- Design projects (such as competitions and other research work) completed outside of school
- Other visual abilities, such as photography, graphic design and drawings

Professional experience
- Make sure to clearly demonstrate your contributions—such as plans you drew, renderings completed or models built

NOTES ON:

EDITING A BAD PROJECT

SHOW PART OF A PROJECT

Some studio projects never mature. But instead of throwing out the whole project, leverage the most successful parts. A great rendering, a decent site diagram and a few strategically cropped plans can make a fair project look lots better.

NOT A GREAT PROJECT, BUT SOME GOOD DRAWINGS

Not your best studio project, but fantastic mappings from an earlier phase of analysis? Show the maps in another part of your portfolio, say under drawings.

LESS IS MORE

Three great images are better than seven. Make sure to edit your work so only the best images remain.

INCLUDING OTHER WORK

INCLUDING OTHER CREATIVE WORK IN YOUR PORTFOLIO demonstrates a breadth of skills. Travel drawings, photographs and graphic design can all be included. However, only include this work if the images demonstrate how you work, rather than just expand the portfolio for the sake of extra material.

Portfolio by Jesse Wilcox

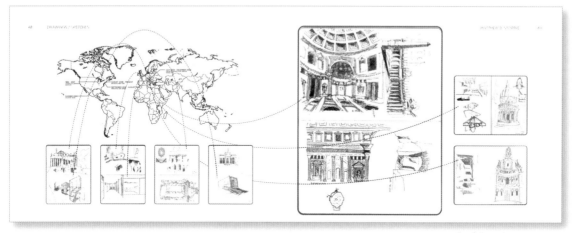

Portfolio by Matthew Storrie

TRAVEL SKETCHES AND PHOTOGRAPHS

As individual sketches, each drawing is sufficient. But showing travel sketches as part of your sketchbook, and part of a larger experience of traveling, studying and drawing makes a rich composition.

POSTERS

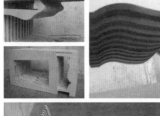

FURNITURE

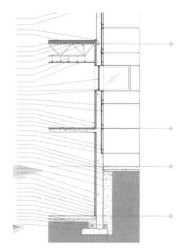

WALL SECTION

GRAPHIC DESIGN

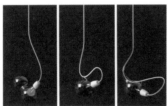

LIGHTING

FASHION

DRAWINGS

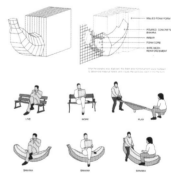

SEATING

DIAGRAM YOUR PORTFOLIO

ORGANIZE YOUR PORTFOLIO CONTENT BY DRAWING A DIAGRAM of page layouts. Visualizing the structure of your portfolio will help you think about pages, pacing and how the book will be organized.

⬇ **BEGINNING PAGES**   ⬇ **ACADEMIC PROJECTS**

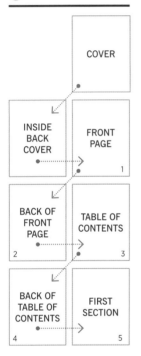

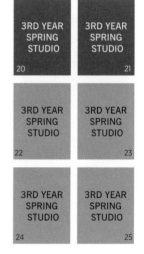

ABOUT THIS DIAGRAM

Layout programs show book pages as a diagram of an open book. The front cover is on the first line (1) as its own right-facing page. The second line of pages shows the inside back cover (2) with the corresponding right-hand page (3).

START WITH YOUR BEST

Reviewers want to see your potential, not your "progress," so start with a great project rather than the project first in your chronology.

SEGUE TO STRONG WORK

Your next few projects should still be good work, but can be slightly fewer pages than the first project.

KEEP MOMENTUM

Emphasize your best projects with the most number of pages while others can be shorter and less detailed.

→ **PAGE TYPES**

Different types of content require different page structures. Think of how different page styles can help pace your portfolio.

Book pages

Intro pages

Project pages

 PROFESSIONAL PROJECTS

BACK OF THESIS PROJECT 40	SECOND SECTION 41

2ND YEAR STUDY 26	2ND YEAR STUDY 27
2ND YEAR STUDY 28	2ND YEAR STUDY 29

HIDE A LESS DEVELOPED PROJECT NEAR THE END

A project that's a good, but perhaps underdeveloped, can be couched right before a strong finale. Limit this project to a few spreads that focus on its best attributes.

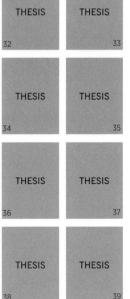

THESIS 30	THESIS 31
THESIS 32	THESIS 33
THESIS 34	THESIS 35
THESIS 36	THESIS 37
THESIS 38	THESIS 39

FINISH STRONGLY

Conclude your academic section with a longer layout of a well-developed, intellectually rich project.

OFFICE WORK 1 42	OFFICE WORK 1 43
OFFICE WORK 1 44	OFFICE WORK 1 45
OFFICE WORK 1 46	OFFICE WORK 1 47

PROFESSIONAL WORK

Design work completed in an office should be clearly separated from your academic work. Make sure there is an obvious distinction between academic and office work.

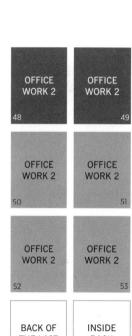

OFFICE WORK 2 48	OFFICE WORK 2 49
OFFICE WORK 2 50	OFFICE WORK 2 51
OFFICE WORK 2 52	OFFICE WORK 2 53

BACK OF THE LAST PAGE	INSIDE BACK COVER
BACK COVER	

GIVE PROPER CREDIT

Only include the professional drawings, renderings and models you worked on.

BOOK PAGES

"BOOK" PAGES ARE PRIMARILY TEXT-BASED. They contain all of the portfolio's "bookish" content such as covers, table of contents, resume and writing samples.

 BOOK PAGES

WHAT THEY ARE

Text-based pages that contain "book-type" content in the portfolio. Book-type pages can be used to design portfolio content such as:

- Table of contents
- Resume or CV
- Research statements
- Writing samples

LOOK OUT FOR

Overdesigning the table of contents. Many students approach the table of contents as a navigation device. A portfolio isn't as complex as a website and doesn't require the same kind of navigation. Stay away from too much color-coding, tabs and bars to structure your work.

Using too many typefaces. You can get a lot of variation out of text by using bold, all caps, light grey, italics or color. One type family can expand into a nuanced yet cohesive palette if you design it right.

Ignoring page margins. Book pages are where most of the "book-like" structure will be most apparent. Since images will be minimal, make sure your organizing grids and margins are closely followed.

Table of Contents

Architecture

01 **Peel for Show**   1-6
New York City Theater Campus

02 **Favela Re[Interpreted]**   7-14
Rio de Janeiro Post-Olympic Housing

03 **Googleplex 2.0**   15-22
Research and Development Complex

04 **Dis[Connected] Market**   23-30
Whole Foods Grocery and North Market

Fabricated Works

05 **[Strip]ple**   31-38
Anthropomorphic Wall Installation

06 **Swiss Army Chair**   39-42
Reconfigurable Multi-Use Furniture Piece

Personal Information

Brian Koehler
Knowlton School of Architecture
The Ohio State University
koehler.130@osu.edu
26852 Dogwood Lane
Perrysburg, OH 43551

Variation of one typeface is created through rigorous and simple changes in the type's weight, scale and color

DESIGNING TEXT

Book pages have a lot of text—table of contents, index, essays—so make sure to consider the way type sits on the page as a set of relationships.

NOTES ON:

TYPOGRAPHY

Typefaces influence the tone and atmosphere of your portfolio. Since the focus should be on your work, shy away from any typefaces that are too "designed," lest they call attention to themselves rather than the work.

CREATE DIFFERENCE

Use one typeface family, but balance bold, black text with lighter grey type.

Irish Town Bend
Cleveland, Ohio

USE INDENTS

Project details are inset from the project title.

SLOW
CURVE
PAOLA ITALY
VISITORS CENTER
FALL 2004 ATLELIER VENICE

SCALE TEXT

Make sure text is scaled to the size of work. Oftentimes text is too large in comparison to the images.

LEFT JUSTIFY

Never justify multiple lines of text to the right. Text to read in a single line can be right justified.

Variation of one typeface is created through rigorous and simple changes in font scale and color

INTRODUCTORY PAGES AND PROJECT PAGES

INTRODUCTORY PAGES ANNOUNCE A PROJECT by creating a visual break in the rhythm and structure of the portfolio and clearly announce that one is in a "new project," while project pages give greater detail about the work. Together these two types of pages structure portfolio pacing.

→ INTRODUCTORY PAGES

Intro pages announce that the reader is looking at a new project and help the viewer orient themselves as they move through the book.

- **Introductory pages announce themselves visually from the rest of the book**

Introductory pages give pacing to the portfolio by also introducing critical project information:

- **Project title and subtitle**
- **Dates and project duration**
- **Team members, project collaborators and instructors**
- **Short description of the project**

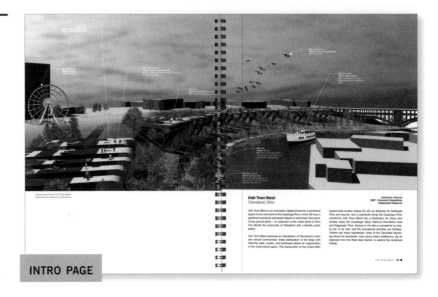

INTRO PAGE

→ PROJECT PAGES

Page spreads that announce a new project. They give pacing to the portfolio by introducing the project with some critical information, and help viewers orient themselves as they move through the book.

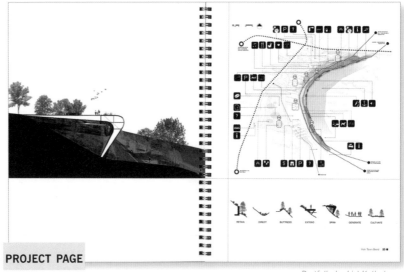

PROJECT PAGE

Portfolio by Lisl Kotheimer

INTRO PAGE

Portfolio by Matthew Storrie

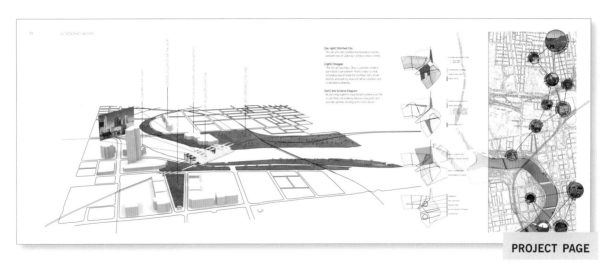

PROJECT PAGE

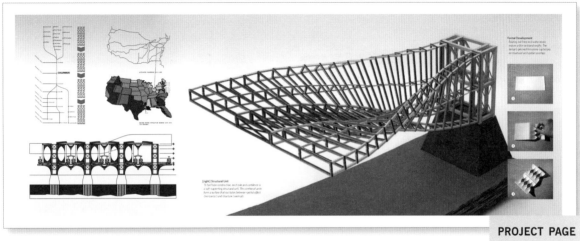

PROJECT PAGE

PORTFOLIO PACING

BOOK PAGES

Text-based pages that contain "book type" content.

INTRO PAGES

Orient the reader to a new project.

PROJECT PAGES

Typical pages that demonstrate the project.

BOOK PAGE

INTRO PAGE

INTRO PAGE

INTRO PAGE

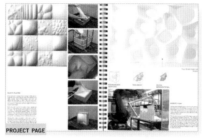

PROJECT PAGE

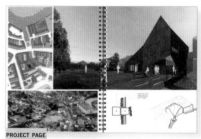

PROJECT PAGE

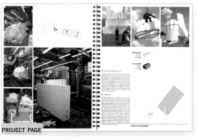

PROJECT PAGE

PROJECT PAGE

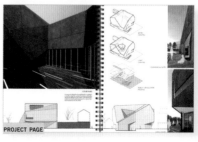

PROJECT PAGE

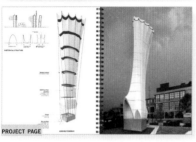

PROJECT PAGE

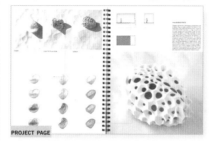

PROJECT PAGE

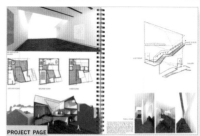

PROJECT PAGE

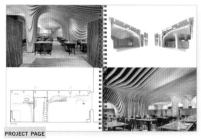

Portfolio by Brandon Clifford

→ **PORTFOLIO CRAFT**

This metal O-ring bound portfolio
slides neatly into a custom-made
portfolio cover.

GRIDS AND GUIDES

GRIDS UNDERLIE EVERY SUCCESSFUL LAYOUT as they keep your text and images organized by giving a structure to place, scale and sequence your work.

MARGINS
Books aren't symmetrical. Take a ruler to your favorite book or magazine and you'll see the margins at the page head are different from the foot, fore and back page edges.

FLOW LINES
Horizontal intervals that help organize page elements. Sometimes they are articulated with a physical line, but often are understood as invisible, consistent guides across the page.

COLUMNS
Divide the page into vertical spaces, and help give text structure and legibility.

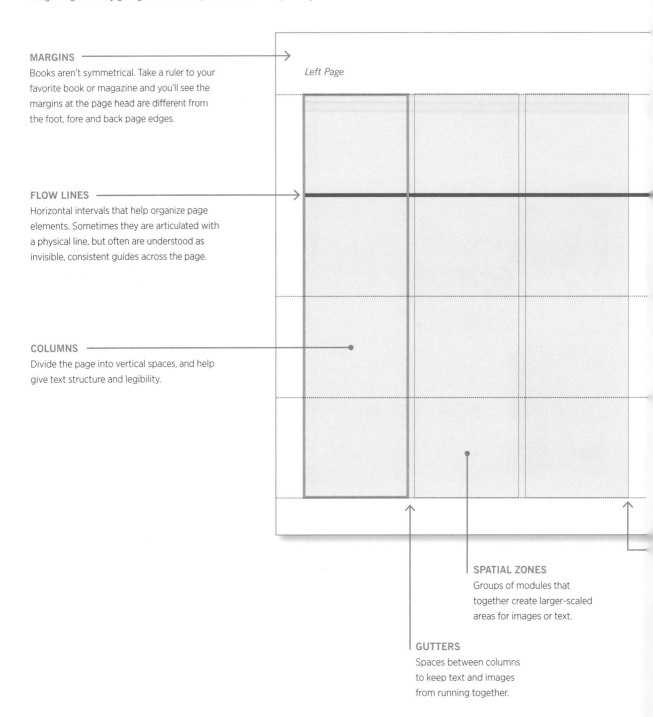

Left Page

SPATIAL ZONES
Groups of modules that together create larger-scaled areas for images or text.

GUTTERS
Spaces between columns to keep text and images from running together.

NOTES ON:

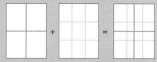

MAKING A GRID

There are endless ways to divide a portfolio page.

HALVES AND THIRDS

In halves   In thirds   Halves and thirds!

A classic grid system that allows for flexibility and proportion.

RECTANGLES AND SQUARES

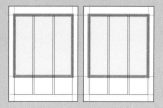

Page = rectangle   Work = square

A nice tension is created between the density of work, presented as a square, and the space of the page.

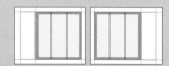

This technique also works when spanning landscape page spreads.

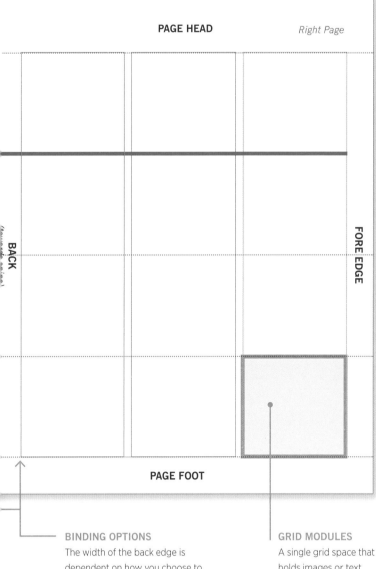

PAGE HEAD   *Right Page*

BACK

FORE EDGE

PAGE FOOT

BINDING OPTIONS
The width of the back edge is dependent on how you choose to bind your portfolio. Coil binding that lays flat? Go all the way to the edge. Perfect binding? Leave a larger space to accommodate page drape.

GRID MODULES
A single grid space that holds images or text.

SAMPLE GRIDS

HALVES AND THIRDS

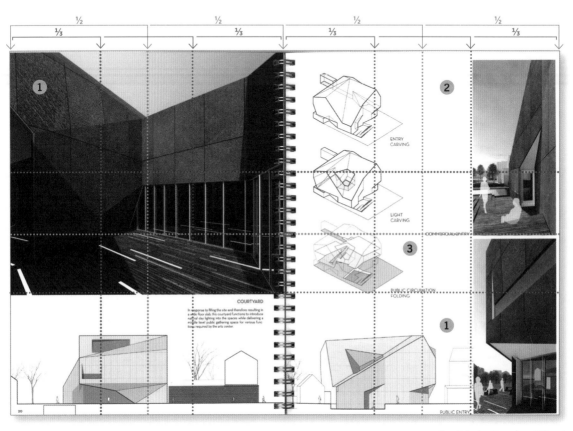

Portfolio by Brandon Clifford

1 SCALE AND DENSITY

The page layout is balanced through darker, saturated renderings and lighter line drawings.

2 LET WHITE SPACE LEAK

If you leave any white space on your page, make sure it isn't "trapped" by images and text.

3 BREAK THE GRID

Not every image is going to fit perfectly within the grid. Adjust the guidelines when your work requires it.

page margins

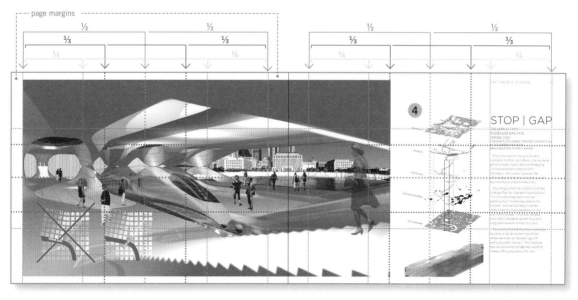

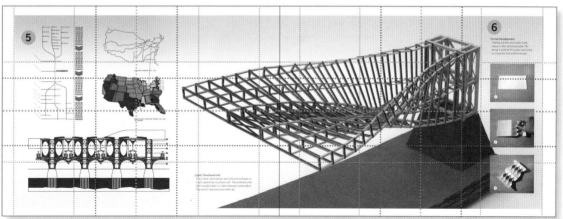

Portfolio by Matthew Storrie

④ EXPANDED PIECES

Small diagrams help explain the project and serve as a nice contrast to information-rich photographs and renderings

⑤ LAYER DIAGRAMS

Adding linework on top of photos or renderings integrates the image into the overall presentation

⑥ DIAGRAM PHOTOS

Photos can also be used to describe a project's development

SAMPLE GRIDS

SQUARES AND THIRDS

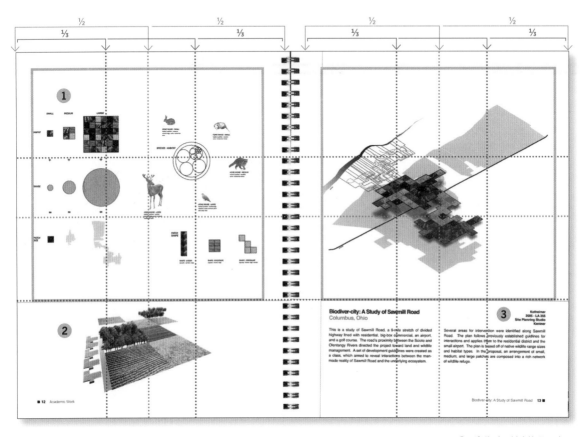

Portfolio by Lisl Kottmeier

1 BIG IMAGES
Large images don't always have to be full-bleed, dense renderings or highly saturated. Light line work can have presence simply by making the images larger.

2 SMALL IMAGES
Don't be afraid to let a rendering be a smaller, detailed image on your page.

3 DENSITY AND DETAIL
Page numbers and other contextual information can add scale and detail to a page layout.

HALVES AND QUARTERS

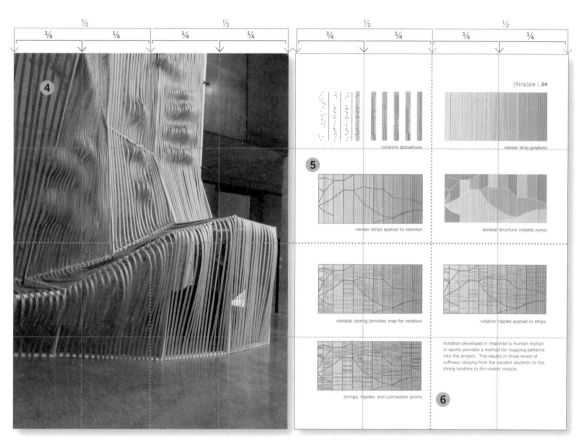

Portfolio by Brian Koehler

4 BLACK AND WHITE

Some images just look better in black and white. The orange wood tones of the thin ply against the cool grey concrete are neutralized when the image is changed to black and white.

5 CONSISTENT COLORS

Diagrams and photos are linked together with a consistent palette (in this case grey, green and blue).

6 THINK IN BLOCKS

Captions and images can work together as a single unit to help organize the page grid.

PORTFOLIO TYPEFACES

COMPRESSING TYPOGRAPHY'S RICH HISTORY AND COMPLEX TECHNICAL details into a few pages is almost impossible. The following is a reductive overview to a few basic principles you need to know to use typefaces effectively.

 THERE ARE TWO* TYPES OF TYPEFACES

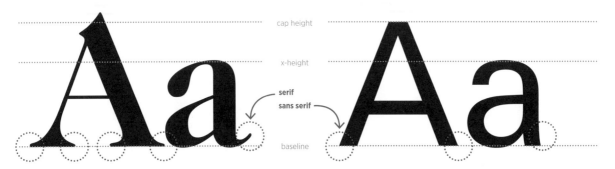

cap height

x-height

serif
sans serif

baseline

↑ SERIF TYPE

The little hooks and lines that extend off of the letters are called "serifs."

WHY THEY ARE GREAT
Serif typefaces are useful for expressing a feeling of **authority, security and establishment**.

The serifs (hooks and lines) help **reinforce the line of the text**, therefore making it easier for your eyes to read the lines.

WHEN TO USE THEM
Serif letters are a good choice for **long stretches of text** that require close reading. Most novels, magazines and newspapers are set in a serif typeface.

SERIF EXAMPLES

Clarendon

Bodoni

Optima

Adobe Caslon Pro

Times New Roman

The Vietnam Memorial used Optima to engrave names on the wall

One of the typefaces used to set this book

↑ SANS SERIF TYPE

"Sans"—French for "without"—indicates that the serifs aren't present on these typefaces.

WHY THEY ARE GREAT
Sans serif typefaces express a sense of **modernity**. Because they are unadorned, they appear **tailored, clean and simple.**

Titles and captions are good places to add **style, color and posture** to a page layout.

WHEN TO USE THEM
Use sans-serif type faces for **titles, subtitles, project information and captions**, or for books when the text is broken into shorter sentences.

SANS SERIF EXAMPLES

Bell Gothic

Futura

Helvetica

News Gothic

Gotham

BREAK THE RULES
All of the suggestions about how to use typefaces are up for grabs. Make your own rules by taking note of how type is used in print, on buildings, anywhere!

TESTING TEXT

Caslon + Univers

The typeface you select sets the tone for your project. Simple changes in color, text size and tracking, and capital letters can change a typeface's tone and feeling. If you're struggling with how to use a typeface, test out a few combinations.

Memory Trail
Flight 93 Memorial Landscape

Friendly

MEMORY TRAIL
Flight 93 Memorial Landscape

Wispy

MEMORY TRAIL
Flight 93 Memorial Landscape

Neutral

This one feels best for a contemporary memorial

MEMORY TRAIL
FLIGHT 93 MEMORIAL LANDSCAPE

Solemn

MEMORY TRAIL
Flight 93 Memorial Landscape

*Neutral, quiet
+
Delicate, happy*

Memory Trail
FLIGHT 93 MEMORIAL LANDSCAPE

*Friendly, happy
+
Solemn*

NOTES ON:

PROCEED WITH CAUTION
Unusual, picturesque typefaces, known as "display type," can express an editorial voice in your portfolio. However, they can be tricky to use. Unless done extremely well, they can distract from—or even ruin!—the atmopshere of the entire portfolio.

KEEP CONTEXT IN MIND
Super expressive typefaces found in magazines, websites and advertising can be very inspiring, but be careful not to get too carried away with stylized typefaces. **Your portfolio is about your architecture work.** Make sure your portfolio design choices support the legibility of your projects. Most magazines that use expressive typography are designing type to editorialize a featured article or fashion spread. Your portfolio is about sharing your work, not a project in expressive typography.

TEXT TYPES

YOUR PORTFOLIO IS A SYSTEM OF PAGE TYPES AND TEXT TYPES. How text is presented can help clarify the way the reader navigates the portfolio, emphasizing project introductions, details and descriptions of each project.

Intro spread is announced with a full-bleed image and introductory text that announces the project

INTRO PAGE

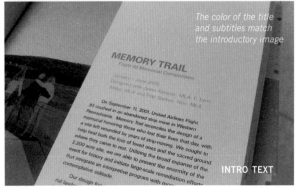

The color of the title and subtitles match the introductory image

INTRO TEXT

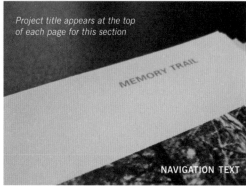

Project title appears at the top of each page for this section

NAVIGATION TEXT

MEMORY TRAIL

Flight 93 Memorial Competition

Phase 1: January 2005
Phase 2: February–June 2005

Collaborators:

Jason Kentner, MLA '04

E. Lynn Miller, MLA '45

Frtiz Steiner, Hon. MLA

On September 11, 2001, United Airlines Flight 93 crashed in an abandoned strip mine in Western Pennsylvania. Memory Trail reconciles the design of a memorial honoring those who lost their lives that day, with a site left wounded by years of strip-mining. We sought to help heal both the loss of loved ones and the sacred ground where they came to rest.

above, left and right:

"Visitor's Center Entrance," Stage 2 Boards

Architecture and overlooks are packaged together to frame significant landscape features

MEMORY TRAIL

DESIGN RESEARCH

Karen Lewis

INTRODUCTORY TEXT

TITLE
Summarizes the project.

SUBTITLE
Gives more illustrative detail.

PROJECT DETAILS
Include any information relevant to the project, such as information about collaborators, project dates and duration and studio critics.

↓ DESCRIPTION TEXT

BODY TEXT
This text will only be read by viewers who thoroughly go through your portfolio. While it's important to pay attention to this text, know that most people will not read this information so make sure the main points are described in title text and captions.

CAPTIONS
Use captions as a way to insert short, significant descriptions of images. Along with project titles, captions are most likely to be read.

NAVIGATION TEXT
At the top or bottom of the page, these elements cue readers into what part of the portfolio they are examining.

HAPPY FAMILIES

All of the "Memory Trail" text is set in the typeface family Univers. Rather than introduce new typefaces, hierarchy is created though different weights, colors, styles and postures.

WOBJ

WILLIAM O'BRIEN JR, PRINCIPAL / CAMBRIDGE, MA

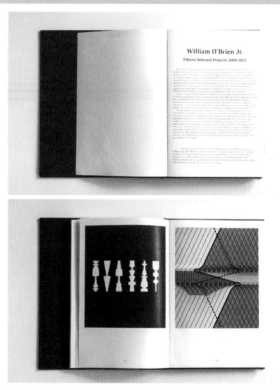

WILLIAM O'BRIEN JR *is Associate Professor of Architecture at MIT School of Architecture and Planning and is principal of WOBJ, an independent design practice in Cambridge, Massachusetts. He is also one of the founding members of Collective–LOK. In 2013 Wallpaper* named his practice one of the top twenty emerging architecture firms in the world. He is the recipient of the 2012–2013 Rome Prize Fellowship in Architecture awarded by the American Academy in Rome. His practice was awarded the 2011 Architectural League Prize for Young Architects and Designers. In 2010 his practice was a finalist for the MoMA PS1 Young Architects Program and was recognized as a winner of the Design Biennial Boston Award.*

GRAPHIC DESIGN FOR ARCHITECTS: How do graphics direct your practice?

WILLIAM O'BRIEN JR: All drawings are abstractions. One has to make choices about what information to include or exclude. If the work is not built, then the only argument one can make is a graphic one. The choices one makes about line-work, which hatches or typefaces one uses—these elements contextualize the work if you're aware of it or not.

As designers, we have to be invested in the graphic quality of the work. The graphic presentation positions the work; it suggests values and affiliations. Those decisions say something about the value-set, the historic affiliations, the cultural context that is motivating the work. To do

that blindly is a missed opportunity. To do that with an awareness of architectural history and all of the representation that come before us is an important way of communicating motivations.

GDA: How did you bring that interest in abstraction into your portfolio collaboration?

WO: We worked with Natasha Jen, now a partner at Pentagram, to develop the portfolio. We had worked together on a project for MIT and I knew her work was quite beautiful, aware and cautious. The work she makes is generic when it needs to be and highly unique when necessary. This approach is in line with our thinking as our practice is interested

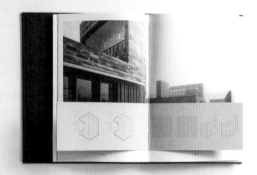

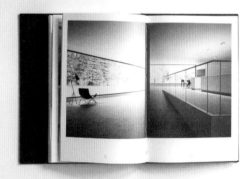

in being specific when we need to be, and almost invisible when we're less interested in making a comment. I was interested in seeing what she would make if I gave her a set of characteristics or requirements for the portfolio. On the one hand, I wanted to see what she would design; but on the other, I wanted to see how she would characterize the work. I wanted to see if she was seeing the same things I was in the work.

GDA: The portfolio became a way to have a conversation, it became a reflection tool.

WO: Yes, a type of feedback. We gave her a difficult task. The words I used to describe the portfolio were words that I think characterize aspects of our design

work such as anachronistic, deadpan, static, forlorn, melancholic. These descriptions seemed challenging to express graphically, but that is how we were thinking about our work. We wanted the project to be more a book than a portfolio, to read more like a novel and less like a conventional, "responsible" architectural portfolio. Instead of moving through spreads of images that tell the reader about the project, we wanted the project text to have equal weight to the visualizations.

We liked the idea of there being an almost anachronistic quality to the book such that the typeface would not be contemporary; the ambition being that the work would be given a quality of timelessness. We didn't want the presentation to make the work look

contemporary. We're not interested in looking contemporary. We wanted the book to feel old; we used symmetry, gutters that are more typical of novels, having fewer images on each page. These elements make it feel like an old book—one which has been and could be relevant for a long time—rather than a book that is aiming to portray the work as "new."

GDA: Why did you decide to work with the graphic designer? Why not do it yourself?

WO: I was interested in what I could learn by working with someone who is not an architect. What could a graphic designer teach me about my work? I had ideas about how I could communicate graphically, but I wanted to learn more

about how a graphic designer would do that. Like all creative disciplines, graphic design has a particular history that every new work speaks to. I wanted the portfolio to be able to participate in earnest within a graphic design discourse.

I was also interested in that ambiguous zone between the graphic and the drawing, and trying to understand the difference between architectural drawing and graphic design. These kinds of cross-disciplinary conversations don't happen unless you make them happen.

I had ideas about what would make a good design portfolio, but I wanted an expert to help guide me. It's one thing to have ideas about graphic design as an architect and it's another to have those ideas validated by a graphic designer who could reflect back to me if the ideas were good or needed to change.

GDA: How did you work together?

WO: I asked Natasha to aim to put into graphic language some of the terminology and characteristics that we had talked through. Given that we all have different ways of thinking about translating qualitative descriptions to concrete design ideas, there was a lot of back and forth about how best to interpret the characteristics we were after.

GDA: The book feels very different from architecture books that, say, use different cropping techniques to communicate movement, to reflect the book's kinetic quality. Were you rejecting these types of techniques?

WO: Maybe our work is oppositional to "kinetics." We use words like deadpan,

static or stoic in discussions about our work, not only because we think our work is like that, but also because we are trying to articulate an opposition to contemporary fascination with dynamism and plasticity. In our work we try to make objects that engaging through static means rather than rely on didactic forms of dynamism to attract attention. We typically think about the projects as sedentary objects—still, but layered objects that prompt more looking. You speak about kinetics and pace—if we were to talk about pace, it would be about slowing down. Putting a single image on a page that might seem too simple to have its own dedicated page, but warrants a discussion of looking closer.

We wanted to do something that's not architecturally responsible. Every architect makes hundreds of drawings about each project and there's often an

effort to include all of the drawings as "proof" you developed a comprehensive project... and we have that desire, too. Yet at the same time, we think that an intelligently distilled drawing has the potential to be as powerful as many conventional architectural drawings. We hope a small set of these types of drawings produces a more compelling argument about the architecture rather than trying to overwhelm in order to convince. We're taking a chance and hoping that the five conceptual drawings will be as cogent as 50 conventional drawings.

GDA: When you place an image on a page, do you ever find that your perception of the drawing begins to change? Does the graphic presentation of the work become a way to confront its qualities?

WO: The graphic quality of the drawing and the page are utterly inextricable. Especially since we happen to be invested in what we could describe as an offshoot of minimalism—a kind of eclectic minimalism. In our case it is critical that we take account of which lines are present, and which are not. There is also a dialogue between the drawing and its captions, its titles, the page numbers. The graphics of type and the graphics of drawing are in no way inseparable.

GDA: Once you place that image on the page or the screen, the layout becomes part of the linework.

WO: Right. And I would also say that attitudes towards drawings change as one's own biases and experiences change. Things look different; you may represent things differently depending on the evolution of your mental state. As an example, before I studied in Rome for a year, I was curious and, perhaps, skeptical about the power of the formal mechanisms of symmetry, proportion, axiality. Now, after being exposed to so many incredibly powerful buildings that utilize these mechanisms so successfully, I crave such formal devices.

I don't think architects talk about this enough. There's usually a conversation about what makes a drawing "correct" for a certain project, but we should be talking about what makes something correct for a certain project at a certain time. Because your values shift, so too do the drawings that represent the values. These things are constantly in flux.

RESUMES

ORGANIZING INFORMATION

THE RESUME IS A PRACTICE IN NESTING INFORMATION. Being able to consume information in a quick, visual way allows for someone to access the resume in two ways: first, quickly as one skims information to get the big picture; and then in a longer, more detailed way to understand fully skills and experiences.

SAME RESUME, DIFFERENT STRUCTURES

Each resume is the same size, uses the same typefaces and includes the same information. Their radically different appearances are a result of space and organization, the basis for all good graphic design projects. **Space, not form, structures the resume.**

Name is too big— emphasize skills and experience instead

Ditch the graphics— use space, rather than heavy lines, to organize information

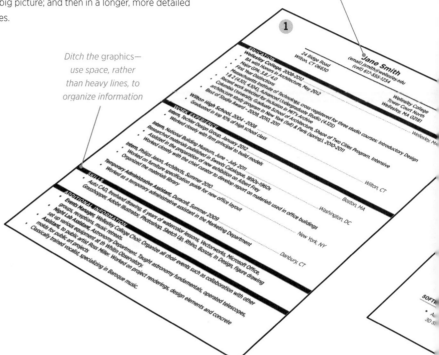

---

1 BAD RESUME

TOO MANY "ELEMENTS"
This resume relies on physical elements such as dark bars, lines and an excessive number of bullet points to organize content. Space, rather than "graphic design" elements, should be used to manage information.

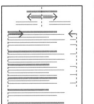

- **Page is imbalanced**
- **Text is set symmetrically, left justified and right aligned**
- **Too many competing elements make the page hard to read, not to mention appear awkward**

2 BETTER RESUME

SIMPLE HORIZONTAL
Larger margins, a baseline grid and simple organizing structures help components fit onto the page. Hierarchies are subtly reinforced with slight indents and larger spaces after sections.

- **Resume content floats away from the page edge**
- **Text is balanced between bold (main info) and light (descriptions) type weights**
- **Subtle indents and flow lines help organize sections**

③ EVEN BETTER RESUME

PACKAGED INFORMATION

Three distinct columns of information help make this resume more easily "skimmed." The overly horizontal quality of a resume is broken apart into three columns that read across and down the page.

- **Center column holds the main descriptions in short, skimmable sentences**
- **Side columns hold ancillary and contextual information**

Name is rescaled and aligned with the rest of the resume

Subtle flow lines and indents give structure to each section

Because the line length is short, information in the center column is highly skimmable. The right column holds information that needs to be quickly scanned, such as relevant skills.

Limit the number of resume sections to three or four—more than this chops up the page

STRUCTURING THE PAGE

THE ORGANIZATION OF YOUR RESUME DEMONSTRATES HOW WELL YOU COMMUNICATE. How you set up the logic of this document shows how you think about your experiences, how well you communicate to others and how clearly you present information.

⬇ FORMING RELATIONSHIPS

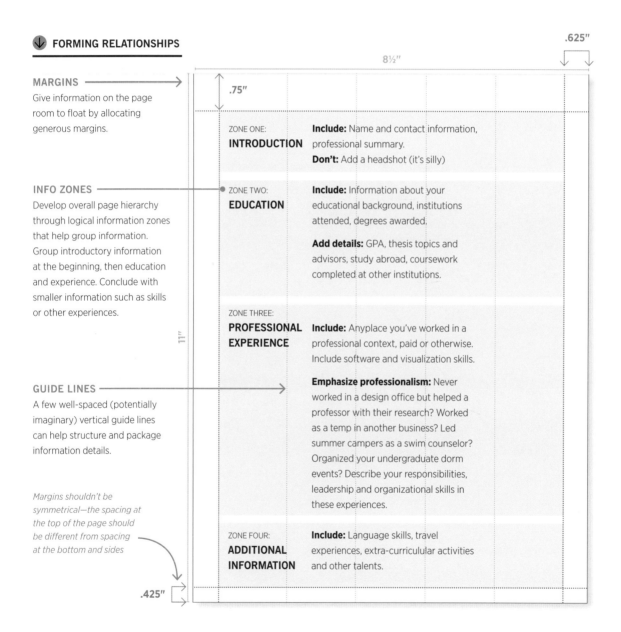

MARGINS
Give information on the page room to float by allocating generous margins.

INFO ZONES
Develop overall page hierarchy through logical information zones that help group information. Group introductory information at the beginning, then education and experience. Conclude with smaller information such as skills or other experiences.

GUIDE LINES
A few well-spaced (potentially imaginary) vertical guide lines can help structure and package information details.

Margins shouldn't be symmetrical—the spacing at the top of the page should be different from spacing at the bottom and sides

.625"

8½"

.75"

11"

.425"

ZONE ONE:
INTRODUCTION
Include: Name and contact information, professional summary.
Don't: Add a headshot (it's silly)

ZONE TWO:
EDUCATION
Include: Information about your educational background, institutions attended, degrees awarded.

Add details: GPA, thesis topics and advisors, study abroad, coursework completed at other institutions.

ZONE THREE:
PROFESSIONAL EXPERIENCE
Include: Anyplace you've worked in a professional context, paid or otherwise. Include software and visualization skills.

Emphasize professionalism: Never worked in a design office but helped a professor with their research? Worked as a temp in another business? Led summer campers as a swim counselor? Organized your undergraduate dorm events? Describe your responsibilities, leadership and organizational skills in these experiences.

ZONE FOUR:
ADDITIONAL INFORMATION
Include: Language skills, travel experiences, extra-curricular activities and other talents.

OTHER ORGANIZATIONS

VERTICAL ZONES

Smaller vertical zones are used to hold ancillary information, such as computer skills, artistic abilities, travel experiences or personal interests. The smaller zones frame the center of the resume, which holds detailed information about professional experiences, leadership and education.

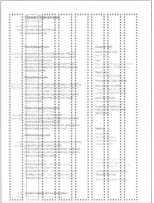

VERTICAL SECTIONS

Experiences are organized into the wider column while skills and personal information are organized into the smaller column.

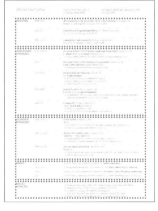

SIMPLE HORIZONTAL

While the resume is organized into horizontal sections, three clear columns organize section headings, dates and experiences.

WHAT FIRMS WANT TO KNOW

EDUCATION

"Put your degree institutions first and foremost. If you attended other schools during a junior year abroad, for example, highlight it under your degree-initiating school, rather than as a separate listing."

CLEAR CHRONOLOGY

"Make the dates easy to read— it's frustrating to track career moves across dates that aren't clearly articulated in the resume."

REFERENCES

"If you're using a reference, especially someone who used to work at our firm, make sure that person knows you're using them as a reference. We had a student apply for a position once using a professor's name without his knowledge—and the professor wasn't eager to give his recommendation."

SOFTWARE SKILLS

"Let us know if there are some programs you're more familiar with than others. **Software packages change so much we're mostly looking for someone with skills that are adaptable."**

59

BASELINE GRID

ONE OF THE MOST CRITICAL TOOLS FOR TYPESETTING, the baseline grid gives proportion and structure to type and spacing. When it's activiated, the baseline grid organizes all of the spaces between text, giving the overall typesetting an organized, proportional feel.

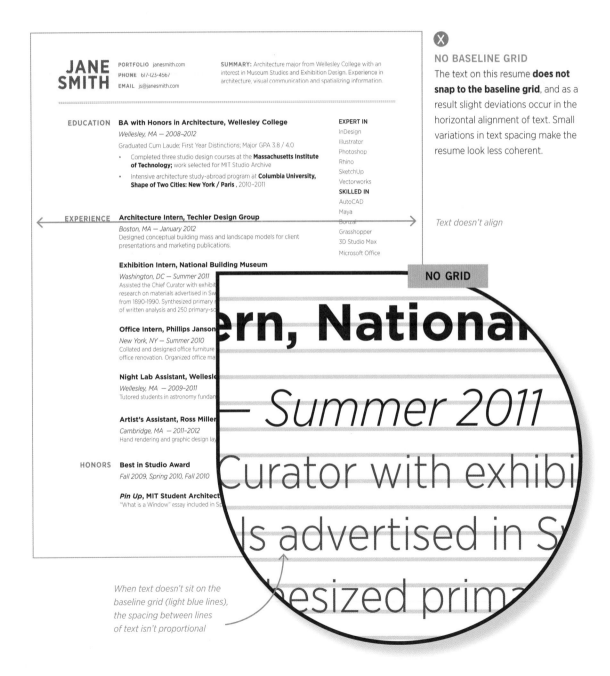

JANE SMITH

PORTFOLIO janesmith.com
PHONE 617-123-4567
EMAIL js@janesmith.com

SUMMARY: Architecture major from Wellesley College with an interest in Museum Studies and Exhibition Design. Experience in architecture, visual communication and spatializing information.

EDUCATION

BA with Honors in Architecture, Wellesley College
Wellesley, MA — 2008–2012
Graduated Cum Laude; First Year Distinctions; Major GPA 3.8 / 4.0
- Completed three studio design courses at the **Massachusetts Institute of Technology;** work selected for MIT Studio Archive
- Intensive architecture study-abroad program at **Columbia University, Shape of Two Cities: New York / Paris** , 2010–2011

EXPERIENCE

Architecture Intern, Techler Design Group
Boston, MA — January 2012
Designed conceptual building mass and landscape models for client presentations and marketing publications.

Exhibition Intern, National Building Museum
Washington, DC — Summer 2011
Assisted the Chief Curator with exhibit
research on materials advertised in Sw
from 1890-1990. Synthesized primary
of written analysis and 250 primary-so

Office Intern, Phillips Janson
New York, NY — Summer 2010
Collated and designed office furniture
office renovation. Organized office ma

Night Lab Assistant, Wellesle
Wellesley, MA — 2009–2011
Tutored students in astronomy fundam

Artist's Assistant, Ross Miller
Cambridge, MA — 2011–2012
Hand rendering and graphic design lay

HONORS

Best in Studio Award
Fall 2009, Spring 2010, Fall 2010

Pin Up, **MIT Student Architect**
"What is a Window" essay included in Sp

EXPERT IN
InDesign
Illustrator
Photoshop
Rhino
SketchUp
Vectorworks
SKILLED IN
AutoCAD
Maya
Bonzai
Grasshopper
3D Studio Max
Microsoft Office

NO GRID

— Summer 2011
Curator with exhibi
ls advertised in S
esized prim

⊗ NO BASELINE GRID
The text on this resume **does not snap to the baseline grid**, and as a result slight deviations occur in the horizontal alignment of text. Small variations in text spacing make the resume look less coherent.

Text doesn't align

When text doesn't sit on the baseline grid (light blue lines), the spacing between lines of text isn't proportional

JANE SMITH

PORTFOLIO janesmith.com
PHONE 617-123-4567
EMAIL js@janesmith.com

SUMMARY: Architecture major from Wellesley College with an interest in Museum Studies and Exhibition Design. Experience in architecture, visual communication and spatializing information.

EDUCATION

BA with Honors in Architecture, Wellesley College
Wellesley, MA — 2008–2012
Graduated Cum Laude; First Year Distinctions; Major GPA 3.8 / 4.0

- Completed three studio design courses at the **Massachusetts Institute of Technology;** work selected for MIT Studio Archive
- Intensive architecture study-abroad program at **Columbia University, Shape of Two Cities: New York / Paris** , 2010-2011

EXPERIENCE

Architecture Intern, Techler Design Group
Boston, MA — January 2012
Designed conceptual building mass and landscape models for client presentations and marketing publications:

Exhibition Intern, National Building Museum
Washington, DC — Summer 2011
Assisted the Chief Curator with exhibition research on materials advertised in Swe from 1890-1990. Synthesized primary re of written analysis and 250 primary-sou

Office Intern, Phillips Janson
New York, NY — Summer 2010
Collated and designed office furniture s office renovation. Organized office mate

Night Lab Assistant, Wellesley
Wellesley, MA — 2009-2011
Tutored students in astronomy fundame

Artist's Assistant, Ross Miller
Cambridge, MA — 2011-2012
Hand rendering and graphic design layo

HONORS

Best in Studio Award
Fall 2009, Spring 2010, Fall 2010

***Pin Up*, MIT Student Architectu**
"What is a Window" essay included in Sprin

EXPERT IN
InDesign
Illustrator
Photoshop
Rhino
SketchUp
Vectorworks
SKILLED IN
AutoCAD
Maya
Bonzai
Grasshopper
3D Studio Max
Microsoft Office

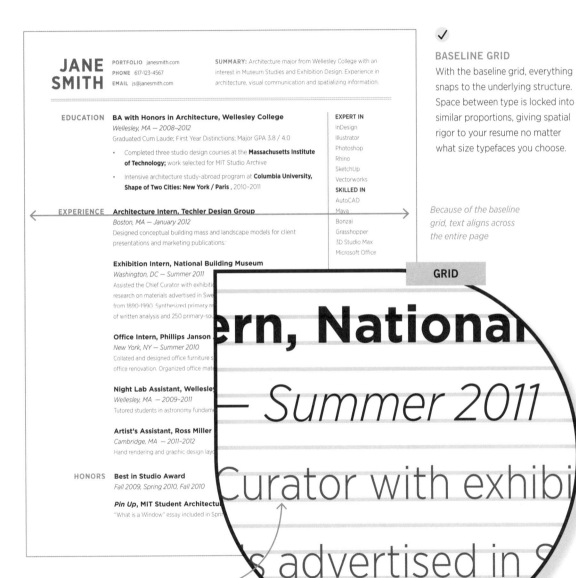

GRID

BASELINE GRID
With the baseline grid, everything snaps to the underlying structure. Space between type is locked into similar proportions, giving spatial rigor to your resume no matter what size typefaces you choose.

Because of the baseline grid, text aligns across the entire page

The bottom of each text line snaps to the grid and spaces between lines of text are even and proportional

NESTING INFORMATION

THE RESUME IS A TRICK OF PACKAGING CONTENT. Being able to consume information in a quick, visual way allows for someone to access your resume in two ways: quickly, as one skims information to get the big picture of experiences; and then in a longer, more detailed way to understand your experiences more fully.

❌ UNPACKAGED INFO

Everything on this resume reads at the same "level." Titles and body text are almost the same weight, and too many graphic elements make it look cluttered.

1 OBJECTIVE

At this stage in your career it's obvious the objective of your resume is to obtain a position. Delete this redundant information.

2 START STRONG

Highlight your relevant experience first rather than the last job you had. If you don't have much work experience, consider starting with leadership experience gained from volunteer positions.

3 TOO MANY "GRAPHICS"

Tone down all of the extra lines and bullet points—too many graphic elements are obtrusive and clutter the resume.

4 WATCH THE MARGINS

Tight margins and wide lines of text make for an awkward layout.

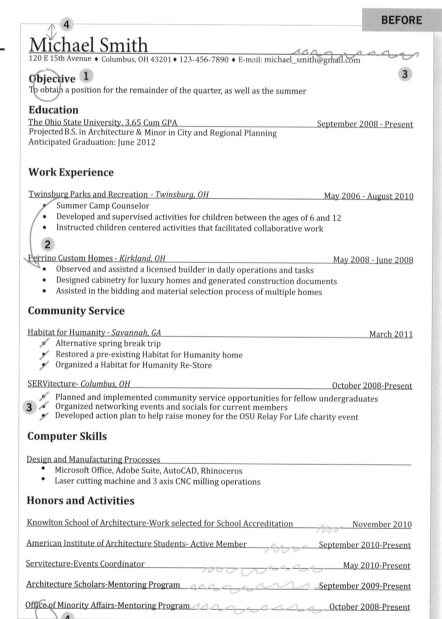

BEFORE

Michael Smith

120 E 15th Avenue ♦ Columbus, OH 43201 ♦ 123-456-7890 ♦ E-mail: michael_smith@gmail.com

Objective 1

To obtain a position for the remainder of the quarter, as well as the summer

Education

The Ohio State University, 3.65 Cum GPA   September 2008 - Present
Projected B.S. in Architecture & Minor in City and Regional Planning
Anticipated Graduation: June 2012

Work Experience

Twinsburg Parks and Recreation - *Twinsburg, OH*   May 2006 - August 2010
- Summer Camp Counselor
- Developed and supervised activities for children between the ages of 6 and 12
- Instructed children centered activities that facilitated collaborative work

Petrino Custom Homes - *Kirkland, OH*   May 2008 - June 2008
- Observed and assisted a licensed builder in daily operations and tasks
- Designed cabinetry for luxury homes and generated construction documents
- Assisted in the bidding and material selection process of multiple homes

Community Service

Habitat for Humanity - *Savannah, GA*   March 2011
- Alternative spring break trip
- Restored a pre-existing Habitat for Humanity home
- Organized a Habitat for Humanity Re-Store

SERVitecture- *Columbus, OH*   October 2008-Present
- Planned and implemented community service opportunities for fellow undergraduates
- Organized networking events and socials for current members
- Developed action plan to help raise money for the OSU Relay For Life charity event

Computer Skills

Design and Manufacturing Processes
- Microsoft Office, Adobe Suite, AutoCAD, Rhinoceros
- Laser cutting machine and 3 axis CNC milling operations

Honors and Activities

Knowlton School of Architecture-Work selected for School Accreditation   November 2010

American Institute of Architecture Students- Active Member   September 2010-Present

Servitecture-Events Coordinator   May 2010-Present

Architecture Scholars-Mentoring Program   September 2009-Present

Office of Minority Affairs-Mentoring Program   October 2008-Present

*Exact same resume, but the
information is presented
better. There is more space
and hierarchy throughout.*

AFTER

Michael Smith
EMAIL: michael_smith@email.com   CELL: 123-456-7890   PORTFOLIO: michaelsmith.com

 EDUCATION

Knowlton School of Architecture, The Ohio State University   *Columbus, OH — 2008-2012*
- Bachelor of Science with Honors in Architecture, Magna Cum Laude; GPA 3.8/4.0.
- Minor, City & Regional Planning
- Design honors: "Best in Studio" award, Winter 2012; Work selected for accreditation, Spring 2011

VOLUNTEER & LEADERSHIP EXPERIENCE

Events Manager, SERVitecture   *Columbus, OH — 2010–2012*
Oversaw event planning for SERVitecture, a community service design organization within the Knowlton School of Architecture.
- Coordinated and planned 7-day spring break trips for Habitat for Humanity
- Developed new fundraiser, "Fashion Shcau" to benefit Dress for Success. Worked with other members to design a university-wide fashion show held at the Knowlton School. Raised $1000.00.
- Organized quartley school-wide promotional events between students and faculty

Volunteer, Habitat for Humanity   *2010-2012*
Participated in various construction and planning activities for Habitat for Humanity, a non-profit construction agency.
- *Cleveland, OH (2012):* Weekend construction and ReStore volunteer for an on-going construction.
- *Savannah, GA (2011):* Lead 10-day spring break trip for 20 KSA students. Constructed homes for five days, worked at the local Re-Store for the rest of the trip. Coordinated with Habitat in Georgia, developed itinerary and managed the budget while traveling.
- *Springfield, OH (2010):* Weekend "blitz-build" to construct two houses in two days.

DESIGN & PROFESSIONAL EXPERIENCE

Research Assistant, Knowlton School of Architecture   *Columbus, OH — March 2012 - present*
Assisted Professor Jane Willis in the development of her book, Architecture for Graphic Designers (Rowledge 2013).
- Researched primary and secondary sources architectural graphic systems such as diagrams, books and maps.
- Created diagrams and produced photographs to be included in the published book.

Logistics Assistant, Ohio State Stores Receiving and Mail   *Columbus, OH — 2011-2012*
Acted as the interface between Ohio State mail customers and Stores logistics network.
- Coordinated package deliveries for university customers with Stores driver fleet.
- Cataloged financial information into university-wide databases, such as PTS, DocFinity and Phoenix.

Camp Coordinator, Twinsburg Summer Camp   *Twinsburg, OH — Summers, 2006-2010*
Senior counselor at 200-person day-camp. Oversaw and trained camp couselors (ages 13-15), worked with children (ages 6-12).
- Developed child centered activities that promoted collaborative work. Sports, swimming, music and art activities.

Senior Studio Project, Perrino Custom Homes   *Kirkland, OH — Spring 2008*
Full-time intern with high-end custom interior design firm focused on trim packages, kitchen design and layouts.
- Developed construction sketches (plans, elevations, details) and material specs for bidding and construction.
- Assisted and observed licensed builder with on-site construction meetings with clients, contractors and sub-specialists.

 SKILLS / INTERESTS

Expert In: AutoCAD; Adobe Illustrator, InDesign, Photoshop; Rhino; Microsoft Office; Laser Cutting
Skilled In: 3D Studio Max, Google SketchUp; 3 Axis CNC Milling
Lanuages: Conversational in Spanish

*Light lines help frame
information without
cluttering the page space*

✓ **COMPLEXITY AND CONTRADICTION**

Ironically, as the organization of the resume becomes more complex, it appears more streamlined. Simplicity requires greater spatial complexity.

1 PAIRING TYPEFACES
Bold, serif typefaces are balanced with light sans serif type. The characteristics complement each other by providing visual weight and relief.

2 GENEROUS SPACING
The baseline grid helps prevent lines of text from jamming up against one another. Indents help package related information, while subtle spaces separate topics.

3 TEXT DETAILS
Only two typefaces are used, but hierarchy is created through different styles for titles, job

4 BETTER MARGINS
A slightly smaller type size allows for better spacing and margins.

MIXING TYPEFACES

TYPEFACES ARE VISUAL SYSTEMS. What kinds of tones are established with their
How typefaces work together visually can help set the tone for your professional work
and create an effective communications environment.

↓ FAMILY DIFFERENCES

Choosing a single typeface and using a family of weights
and postures—bold, book, light, italic—can create hierarchy
while still maintaining continuity.

Jason Kentner —→ *News Gothic, Bold, 17pt*
22 Putnam Avenue ——————→ *News Gothic, Light, 7.5pt*
Cambridge, MA 02139
(cell) 617-555-1234

REED HILDERBRAND ——→ *News Gothic, Bold, 9pt*
Office Associate ——————→ *News Gothic, Bold, 9pt*
1998–2001 ——————————→ *News Gothic, Light, 7.5pt*

WHY THIS IS GREAT
• Keeps the graphic quality consistent
• Differences are created through nuance

LOOK OUT FOR
Maintaining difference. If you choose to work with
a single typeface, make sure you have enough of
the family to build hierarchy and difference between
typefaces. Bold against light provides better hierarchy
than roman against light.

Jason Kentner
22 Putnam Avenue
*Balancing type scale, bold and
light weights provide hierarchy*

Jason Kentner
22 Putnam Avenue
*Roman and light are too
similar—not enough difference*

↓ PAIRING SIMILAR TYPEFACES

Some sans serif typefaces are square and flat, others tall
and fluid. Mixing stylistic choices helps balance the pacing
of dense content, allowing information to be more easily
understood.

JASON KENTNER *Futura Bold, 13pt*
22 Putnam Avenue————→ *Gotham Narrow Light,*
Cambridge, MA 02139 *8pt, tracking +25*
(cell) 617-555-1234

Reed Hilderbrand ——————→ *Futura Bold, 9pt*
OFFICE ASSOCIATE ——————→ *Futura Bold, 6pt*
1998–2001 ——————————→ *Gotham Narrow Light,*
8pt, tracking +25

WHY THIS IS GREAT
• Slight stylistic allow for another texture to be added
  while still maintaining similar stylistic profile
• Maintains a modern tone

LOOK OUT FOR
Slight adjustments. When using similar typefaces,
legibility resides with the details. Because the fonts look
proportionally similar, small adjustments in tracking and
spacing differences can yield significant results, making
information easier to see.

JASON KENTNER *No adjustments to*
.5″ 22 Putnam Avenue *the horizontal or*
Cambridge, MA 02139 *vertical alignments*
(cell) 617-555-1234
.8″

JASON KENTNER
.6″ 22 Putnam Avenue *Legibility increases*
Cambridge, MA 02139 *with more leading and*
(cell) 617-555-1234 *tracking, especially*
.95″ *between the numbers*

↓ PAIRING SERIFS AND SANS SERIFS

Pair serif and sans serif typefaces by considering their properties. Thin and simple Futura pairs well with intricate Sentinel. The narrow "n's" in Bodoni have a similar stance as those in FF Din. Look for commonalities and contrasts to provide rhythm.

SENTINEL + FUTURA

Jason Kentner
22 Putnam Avenue
Cambridge, MA 02139
(cell) 617-555-1234

Reed Hilderbrand
Office Associate
1998–2001

JASON KENTNER
22 Putnam Avenue
Cambridge, MA 02139
(cell) 617-555-1234

REED HILDERBRAND
Office Associate
1998–2001

CASLON + UNIVERS

Jason Kentner
22 Putnam Avenue
Cambridge, MA 02139
(cell) 617-555-1234

Reed Hilderbrand
Office Associate
1998–2001

Jason Kentner
22 Putnam Avenue
Cambridge, MA 02139
(cell) 617-555-1234

Reed Hilderbrand
Office Associate
1998–2001

CLARENDON + TRADE GOTHIC

Jason Kentner
22 Putnam Avenue
Cambridge, MA 02139
(cell) 617-555-1234

Reed Hilderbrand
Office Associate
1998–2001

Jason Kentner
22 Putnam Avenue
Cambridge, MA 02139
(cell) 617-555-1234

Reed Hilderbrand
Office Associate
1998–2001

BODONI + FF DIN

JASON KENTNER
22 Putnam Avenue
Cambridge, MA 02139
(cell) 617-555-1234

REED HILDERBRAND
Office Associate
1998–2001

Jason Kentner
22 Putnam Avenue
Cambridge, MA 02139
(cell) 617-555-1234

Reed Hilderbrand
Office Associate
1998–2001

↓ NOTES ON:

WHAT THE FONT?

"I love your poster design! Which font did you use?" Argh! Font? Font?! *Sigh.* "Oh, you must mean **typeface**."

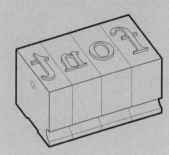

FONTS DELIVER

Saying "font" instead of "typeface" is a common mistake. **Fonts are the delivery mechanism**—computer files, wooden blocks or cases of metal pieces—of a stylized collection of letters and numbers.

TYPEFACES HAVE STYLE

The specific styling of the collection is the typeface. When we appreciate beautifully designed letters on a poster, we are enjoying the visual style of the typeface.

FONTS = MP3s

Asking "Which font did you use?" is akin to asking "I love this music! Which MP3 is playing?" As we know, MP3s are just the delivery mechanisms for the songs we love. The same is true for fonts, which are just the delivery mechanism for the typeface.

Fonts : Typefaces = MP3s : Songs

BENJAMIN VAN DYKE

GRAPHIC DESIGNER / MICHIGAN

1

BENJAMIN VAN DYKE *is part of the faculty in the Department of Art, Art History and Design at Michigan State University and Vice President of DesignInquiry—a non-profit design collective focused on research and education. Van Dyke's work focuses on an experimental approach to typography through site-specific installations. He has been invited to exhibit his work across North America, Europe, Asia and the Middle East and continues to read, write and create works that increase our capacity for a state of benevolent flux.*

GRAPHIC DESIGN FOR ARCHITECTS: Your work with typography is spatial and structural—how do those ideas organize your work?

BENJAMIN VAN DYKE: Space and structure are primary elements of the work as a translation of graphic design. My work explores materials and space, but it also is trying to tap into the essence of communication. What is communication, what does it mean? And how does it perform on a level that is much more subtle, nuanced and complex than the typical communication structures to which we have become accustomed?

GDA: What is the typical role of communication in graphic design? How does your work challenge those communication conventions?

BVD: The typical role of the graphic designer as communicator is to be a linear conduit of transferring an idea from one entity to another as simply and clearly as possible. I do think there is a space for that role. I think the majority of graphic designers in the world are trained to be this type of translator and, in most contexts, that's very efficient and very good. Especially if you're designing, say, signage for a highway on ramp.

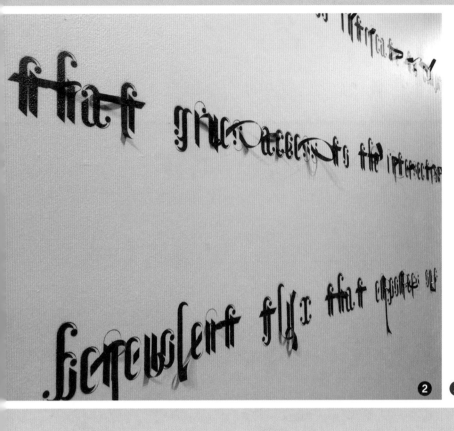

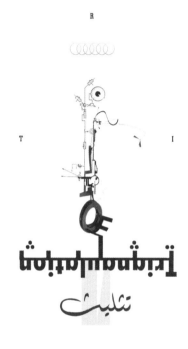

2 **3**

However, in my work, I'm interested in exploring when communication doesn't work so efficiently. When I was a young art director, I was frustrated with the fact that everything had to be incredibly simple, transparent and linear. Interrupting that pattern meant producing risk and most clients aren't interested in paying for communication risks. Our work had become so predictable started implementing these little moments of disturbance into the work. I'm trying to create relevance for complexity in communication. As we know, communication itself is a series of fairly simple patterns. If they weren't simple, we wouldn't be able to communicate. However, we as human beings are not simple beings. We are very, very complex beings—we don't have the innate capacity to understand how complex we actually are. For us to create redundant visual communication patterns is problematic because I believe this creates a visual culture completely opposite who we actually are. I think simplicity creates numbness towards complexity.

GDA: There is a lot about the world that's inherently complex—to the point where clarification can be a creative act.

BVD: One of the ways I try to contextualize conversations about complexity is through an idea I call "benevolent flux." It's a way of trying to explain the value of change, randomness and uncertainty and how it can be implemented in positive, innovative ways.

I had a discussion with a client who hired me based on previous design work. When I presented my ideas to him, the client was upset claiming, "No one will understand it. We can't read the type, it's not legible." I say *everyone* will understand it, it *is* legible. The work is a little bit striking. There is a visual barrier that slows people down a little bit, but people will read it and understand the work. Chaos tends to slow people down and control tends to speed people up.

GDA: You are free to explore these issues of legibility in your installations.

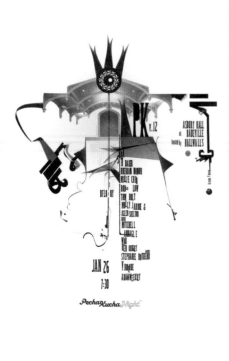

BVD: The gallery has always been an exciting space. I love doing exhibitions because it lets the gallery become a laboratory. As a designer, there's already a sort of disconnect in this space—it isn't traditional for a designer to be working in a gallery. There's also an assumption that when someone walks into the gallery, they are more open minded than in other places. The moment typography is introduced, people instantly see letters and believe there's something to be learned. There's data in this structure. Because of this, you can bring people into the work very quickly. They're open minded already because there appears to be something gleaned from the experience.

I am vigilant about making sure the visitor knows this exhibition is coming from a graphic designer. Without that categorization, they assume sculpture. But I want people to bring their interpretations of design into the room. When the work doesn't make any sense to you, that's the moment when I feel that I am speaking.

GDA: In your work, how does materiality influence communication?

BVD: I haven't quite figured this out—I think it has something to do with coming of age in the late 1990s when Computer Aided Digital Design was at its highest, newest point. Apple was cornering the market of designer technology. And as a result these digital tools created a massive wave of very flat, very pasty design. I had a reaction to that. It felt inauthentic. I didn't want to make flat work and I struggled with this. I was in grad school when I started experimenting with metal, wax, plastic, anything I could pull apart. In some ways it was a metaphor for what I wanted to do with language—to pull it apart and find its breaking point. I had started welding, working with metals, and made big three-dimensional pieces. It felt very liberating. I also met and spoke with the artist Arthur Ganson whom I saw speak when I was in graduate school. He really inspired me. After that meeting, the computer felt shallow. I was obsessed with feeling the things I was designing.

GDA: Why are you trying to liberate typography? Why reinvent it with physical, material qualities?

College of Arts and Sciences
University at Buffalo *The State University of New York*

THE DEP**ART**MENT OF VISUAL STUDIES PRESENTS A LECTURE BY JULIETTE YUAN, BEIJING-BASED CURATOR AND WRITER

袁小漾 Juliette Yuan

WEDNESDAY APRIL 25, 4:30p, CFA B13

6

BVD: I'm searching for new levels of understanding. I'm looking for language that is beyond communication—for other ways of knowing. I want to know where the line is between chaos and control.

I have a technique to explain this concept to students. I draw a line on the chalkboard. On the left side is chaos, on the right is control. If we are redesigning a stop sign, we need to be on the side towards control. If it's a band's next album, we lean towards the chaotic. It's a nonlinear path. It's not here or there, black or white, fast or slow. It's a combination of those things. It's such a combination that we may not have the ability to comprehend this—it is "cha-ordic." As a designer, if you can understand how to be on both sides, you can play the entire field. It's a way to be successful.

GDA: If chaos is one side and order is on the other, what is moving between these forces? Innovation?

BVD: Moving between chaos and control is *learning*. Knowledge is something we've already determined to be true. But learning is more chaotic. Benevolent flux is about considering complexity as a realistic virtue. Instead of keeping chaos, uncertainty or risk under control, I want to recognize that creating new knowledge requires great risk.

↑ **VISUAL BARRIERS**

1: Contaminated Patterns
Mansfield University, Pennsylvania

2–3: EAST/WEST/EAST
*BKE Gallery, Amman, Jordan.
With Hamza Najjar*

4: Pecha Kucha 12: Buffalo

5: Untangle Me
*Banvard Gallery,
The Ohio State University*

6: Juliette Yuan Lecture:
University at Buffalo.
*"Insight" font designed
by Kelsey Leach*

PRESENTING WORK

COMPETITIONS

STRUCTURING THE ARGUMENT

WHEN YOU ORGANIZE THE PAGE, YOU ORGANIZE THE ARGUMENT. How you set up the logic of the competition board is based on the logic of the narrative you are presenting. While this skill is always important in architecture, it is especially significant in competitions when you're not in the room to present the project.

The grid used for this competition board is based on the smallest unit of the board—the diagram monocle

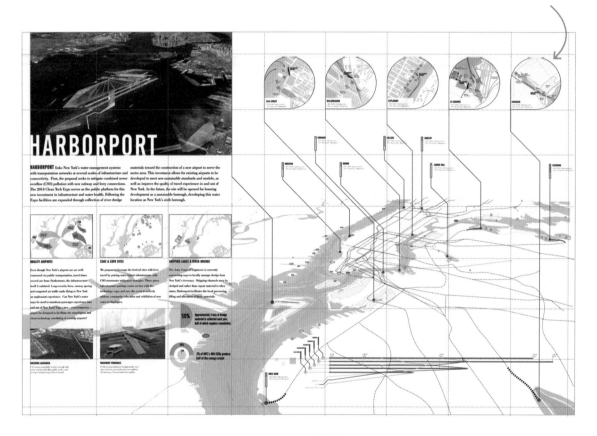

⬆ BOARD ONE: VISUALIZE RESEARCH

The first competition board establishes the context that the proposal is addressing. Diagrams and caption titles focus on three things: airports, water pollution and river dredge. Renderings on the first board give an image of how sustainable water infrastructure can impact transportation planning.

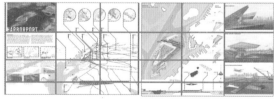

GRID STRUCTURES

Images, text, diagrams and plans are organized on the page to graphically relate to one another. This graphic organization helps frame the argument, prioritizing which images promote ideas.

⬇ BOARD TWO: IMPLEMENT STRATEGY

The second board shows how airports, river dredge and CSOs come together to establish the proposal. Plans, phasing diagrams and atmospheric renderings demonstrate how the strategy is implemented.

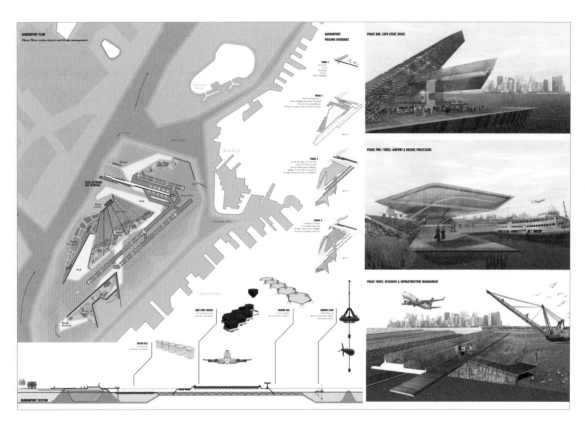

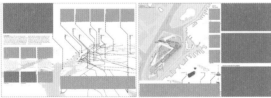

Board imagery becomes cohesive through a color palette—similar colors help the saturated renderings visually relate to the light linework of the plans, sections and diagrams

IMAGE DENSITY

The board is balanced with larger linework images (plans), medium-density images (perspective drawings) and smaller diagrams (information graphics, sections). Balance small, medium and large images with dense renderings and lighter linework.

SCALES OF INFORMATION

THE
GENERAL STORE

HISTORIC PRECEDENT

PROGRAM
The general store acted as the main mixed-use space in countless small towns. It carried all the products people needed in their daily lives and acted as the local post office guaranteeing customers.

PORCH
Nearly all general stores had a porch as their main public face. As people would pick up their mail and other goods they would stop on the porch and chat with other residents.

SITE STRATEGY
TAKE 1 UNDERUTILIZED SEMI-PUBLIC BUILDING...

BECAUSE OF RESTRICTIVE zoning codes, the one non-residential building found in most subdivisions is a private community center, such as a pool house. The Suburban General Store is inserted into these underused structures to become functional centers within each subdivision.

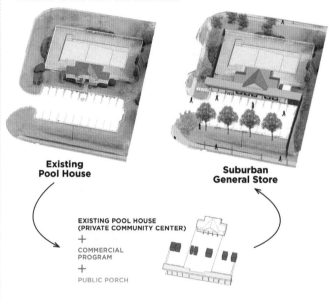

Existing Pool House

Suburban General Store

EXISTING POOL HOUSE
(PRIVATE COMMUNITY CENTER)
+
COMMERCIAL PROGRAM
+
PUBLIC PORCH

PROGRAM STRATEGY
... ADD A PC
A MIX OF P

THE PUBLICLY-CONSTRUC
a balanced mix of uses and ele
and benefits within the subdivi

PUBLIC PORCH AS INFRASTRUCTURE

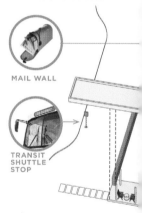

MAIL WALL

TRANSIT SHUTTLE STOP

PRIVATE PLUG IN PROGRAMS

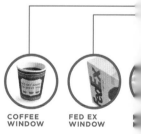

COFFEE WINDOW

FED EX WINDOW

BLEND WITH
AMS

ivately-operated Suburban General Store consists of
o generate the maximum foot traffic, local suport

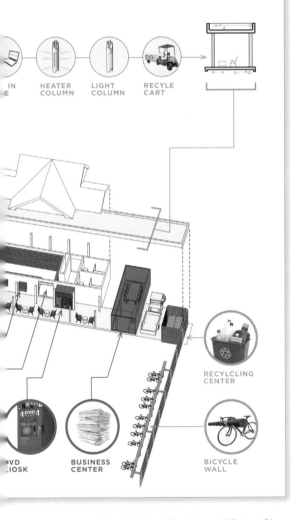

RECYLCLING
CENTER

VD
IOSK

BUSINESS
CENTER

BICYCLE
WALL

HEATER
COLUMN

LIGHT
COLUMN

RECYCLE
CART

IN
E

Project by Frank Ruchala and Michael Piper

1 SCALED TEXT

The project title is given
prominence at the top of
the board, but is scaled so
it acts as a contextualizing
reminder and doesn't
overwhelm the board.

2 INFORMATION TITLE

Text can clearly lay out
the argument, giving
context to the drawings
that demonstrate the
proposal. "Site strategy"
is a sub-header to "Take 1
underutilized semi-public
building….," a bold statement
that helps situate the
drawings.

3 SUPPORTING INFO

Historic context and images
are placed to the side of
the main presentation,
providing support to the
main argument. Images and
text are smaller and black
and white to act as captions
for the main idea.

4 LINES SEPARATE

Light graphic lines help
separate arguments and
keep images grounded to
the page.

↓

NOTES ON:

CONSISTENT
COLORS

COMPLEMENTARY COLORS

Throughout the board, public
programs and infrastructures are
coded with blue, while private
sponsorships are red.

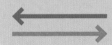

COLORED LINES

Different drawing types—axons,
sections and diagrams, for
example—are visually connected
to one another through colored
lines that help expand the story.
For example, blue lines show
more information about the public
investment as well as connecting
different drawing types to one
another. Blue captions connect
elements, too.

COMPOSING ELEMENTS

The board is balanced with larger
linework images (plans), medium-
density images (perspective
drawings) and smaller diagrams.

LAYERING INFORMATION

COMPRESSING INFORMATION CAN CLARIFY YOUR ARGUMENT. Sometimes more complex and layered information can be easier to follow than singular, isolated pieces. Layered images can create different scales of information.

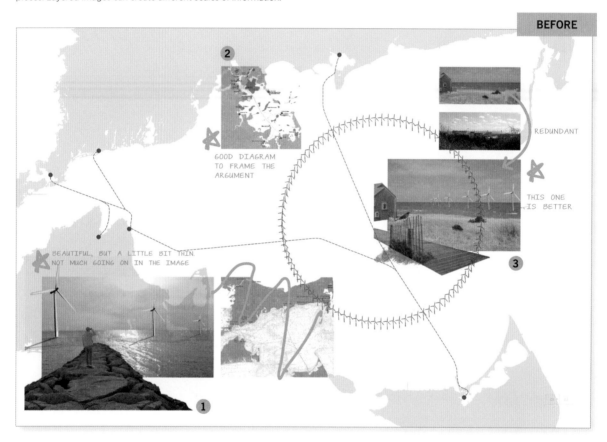

BEFORE

GOOD DIAGRAM
TO FRAME THE
ARGUMENT

REDUNDANT

THIS ONE
IS BETTER

BEAUTIFUL, BUT A LITTLE BIT THIN.
NOT MUCH GOING ON IN THE IMAGE

1 RUN TO THE EDGE

Not every image has to expand to the page edge, or be organized against the edge of the page.

2 SEQUENCING IMAGES

Images should support the argument you want to make, not necessarily the sequence of when the images were made. Consider how the order of images impacts the board design.

3 MISSING HIERARCHY

If all of the images are about the same size, it's hard to enter the argument. Give priority to the discussion by making some images larger and others smaller.

✓ **IMAGE HIERARCHY**

In this edited presentation board, information is made clear by compressing ideas into maps and diagrams. Ironically, making information more visually dense makes the message easier to read.

AFTER

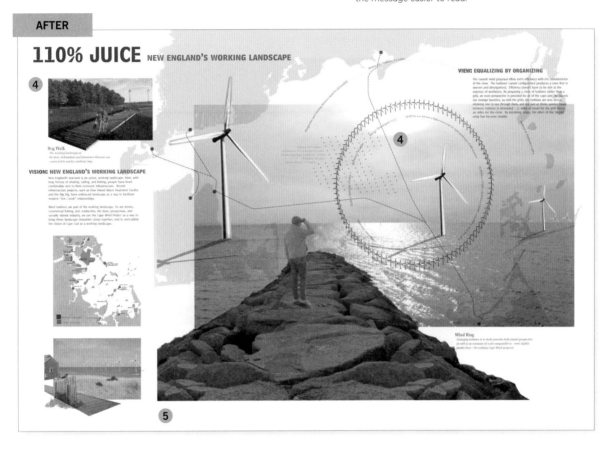

4 TITLE / IMAGE / CAPTION
Visually linking the project title with an emblematic image helps the reader enter the argument. Captions reinforce the wider concepts.

5 LINE IT UP
A band of contextualizing information holds the beginning of the page, giving a space for details that support the larger perspective.

6 LAYER IMAGES
Don't hesitate to layer diagrams on top of perspective renderings, especially when they directly relate to each other.

ORGANIZING IMAGES

COMPETITIONS ARE EXERCISES IN COMMUNICATION which negotiate design expectations with the jury's sensibilities. Ideas competitions demand a high level of speculation and creativity, while a competition with multiple phases requires growth and development if selected to the next stage.

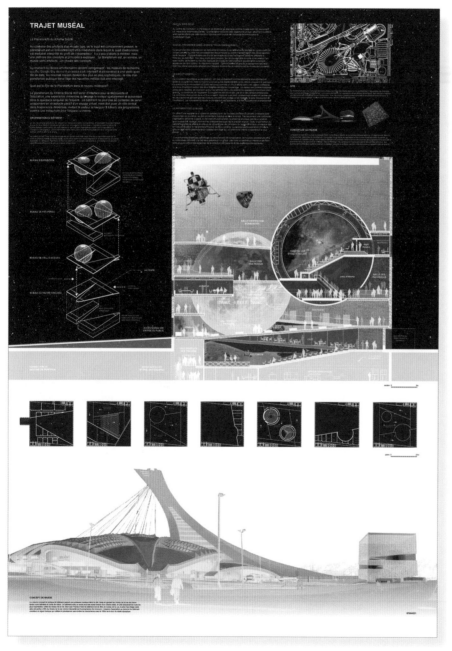

Elijah Huge

FIGURE GROUND

The section for this project is placed uncharacteristically at the center of the board. By presenting the section centrally and at such a large scale, the board is effectively divided into two zones. The zone above uses the background imagery to hold explanations, site information, precedent and diagrams about the project, while the lighter zone at the bottom demonstrates the material organization and appearance of the project.

Colored hatch grounds the drawing without overwhelming the project detail

Typical block configuration

Project proposal

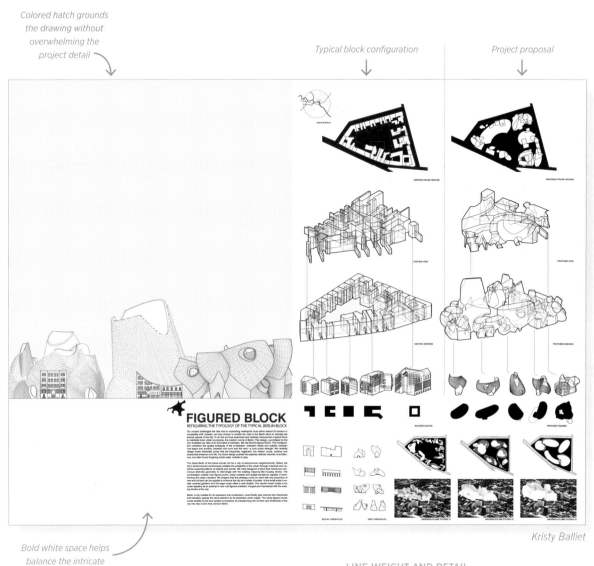

FIGURED BLOCK
REFIGURING THE TYPOLOGY OF THE TYPICAL BERLIN BLOCK

Kristy Balliet

Bold white space helps balance the intricate project linework

LINE WEIGHT AND DETAIL

Complex figures benefit from black and white lineweight-heavy images. The representation technique allows the project's form to be best understood, while keeping the tone of intricacy and detail. The board layout is clean and simple, allowing the viewer a broad overview of the project while also inviting a closer look.

MIXING DRAWING TYPES

SUCCESSFUL PRESENTATION BOARDS LAYER DIFFERENT TYPES OF DRAWINGS.
Site photos, text, maps, perspectives, plans and diagrams are organized through a project narrative. Rather than put all of the plans on one board, for example, and all of the perspective renderings on another, the best presentation boards emphasize project narrative rather than types of drawings.

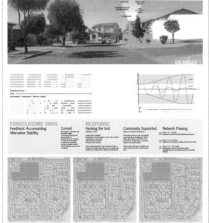

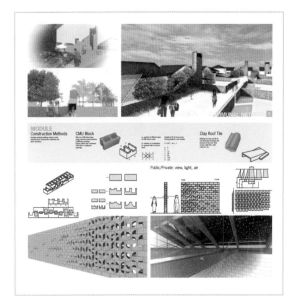

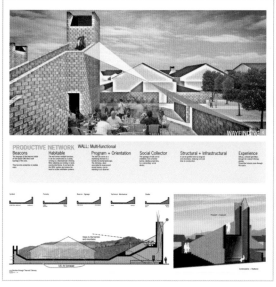

The center of this perspective drawing is darker than the edges

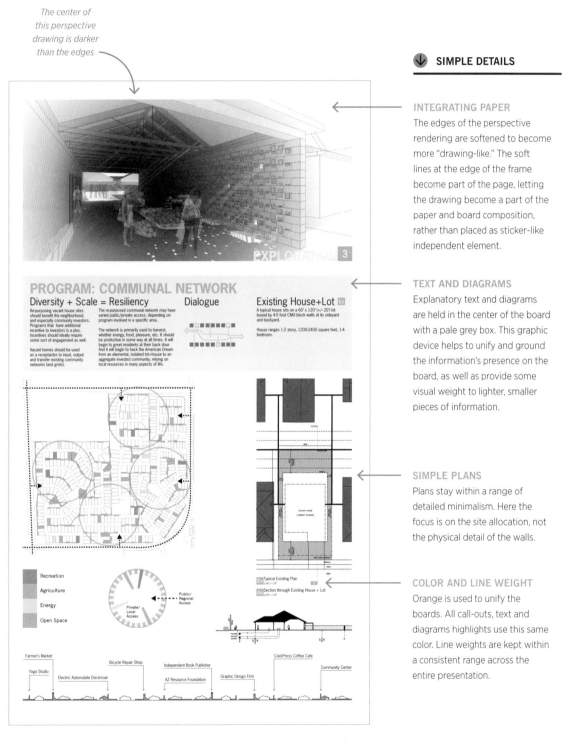

SIMPLE DETAILS

INTEGRATING PAPER
The edges of the perspective rendering are softened to become more "drawing-like." The soft lines at the edge of the frame become part of the page, letting the drawing become a part of the paper and board composition, rather than placed as sticker-like independent element.

TEXT AND DIAGRAMS
Explanatory text and diagrams are held in the center of the board with a pale grey box. This graphic device helps to unify and ground the information's presence on the board, as well as provide some visual weight to lighter, smaller pieces of information.

SIMPLE PLANS
Plans stay within a range of detailed minimalism. Here the focus is on the site allocation, not the physical detail of the walls.

COLOR AND LINE WEIGHT
Orange is used to unify the boards. All call-outs, text and diagrams highlights use this same color. Line weights are kept within a consistent range across the entire presentation.

Aaron Frazier

DUB STUDIOS

MICHAEL PIPER, PRINCIPAL / TORONTO, ON

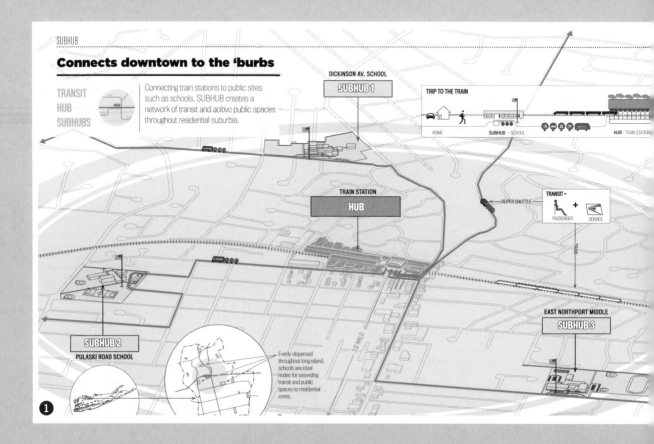

MICHAEL PIPER *is a principal at dub Studios—an architecture and urban design practice in New York and Los Angeles—and on the faculty at University of Toronto. Piper studies the form and organization of contemporary metropolitan regions. His work creates legible analysis of complex urban organizations, and translates these analytics into practicable techniques that engage architecture and city. His work has won or placed in several design competitions and participated in symposia that address American suburbs and contemporary metropolitan regions.*

GRAPHIC DESIGN FOR ARCHITECTS: You're deeply interested in suburban form— what representation methods do you use to study these sites?

MICHAEL PIPER: We apply an interest in systems diagramming to formal conditions in dispersed urban areas. We seek to understand these areas by studying the ordinary building types that systematically repeat across an expansive area.

Frank Ruchala and I first worked with this method in a competition entry we called the *Suburban General Store.* Many of Atlanta's residential subdivisions have pool houses at their center, known oxymoronically in zoning parlance as *private community*

centers. We proposed to layer on a series of private programs and public services into these quasi-public structures, and affectionately named it a general store. At first we tried to represent all of these new and diverse infrastructures with a kind of graphic complexity. Tom Alberty, an incredibly talented graphic designer, started work on the project and immediately helped us pare down the ideas into discernible layers. With Tom's method of graphic design, the complexity of the new infrastructural systems was communicated, but not at the expense of our initial idea.

As an architect, I've always been interested in telling stories, in creating as clear a picture as possible of the mess

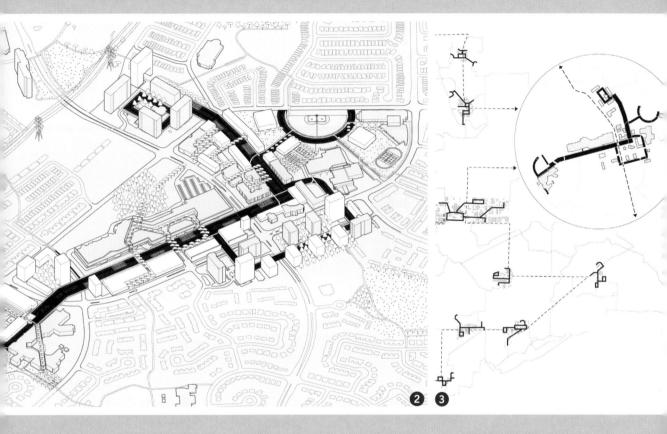

that often comes with doing building projects. While I've always thought myself a pretty good storyteller, Tom showed me how to structure information to allow big ideas and supportive details to coexist. The overall structure of the *Suburban General Store* graphics is pretty straightforward, almost dumb, but more intelligence is layered on the closer you look.

GDA: Does your interest in legibility relate to your practice of working at larger architectural and urban scales?

MP: Clarity certainly becomes more important the larger a project gets—both in terms of physicality and constituencies. As more stakeholders become involved, legibility becomes increasingly important.

I think that, for a long time, architecture as a practice has tended towards visually manifesting the conditions of society. As cities became more spread out and complex after the 1970s, there seemed to be a desire to represent that complexity. I understand why this happened, but, as an alternative practice, we have a desire to not just represent the complex conditions of culture but to somehow engage with them directly, to make the underlying logic of complexity more legible.

GDA: A practice of engaging culture, rather than representing it, requires another type of visual and rhetorical structure. A way of making arguments.
MP: Yes, I think so. For a long time the suburbs, or dispersed metropolitan

areas, seemed formally too complex to think of in physical terms. The term *sprawl* comes from a frustration at the apparent illegibility of its form. Sharing this frustration, our first suburban designs worked on these areas through their infrastructure and other organizational systems—looking at commuting patterns, transportation networks or particular building typologies—as sites for intervention. Through this process, though, we discovered that there is a logic and organization to the suburbs that guide their physical form.

With *Highway Overlay,* a project I did during a fellowship at Ohio State, I studied zoning as a system for effecting form. This research looked at Columbus Ohio's form-based zoning code (a popular New Urbanist tool) and critiqued the relevance

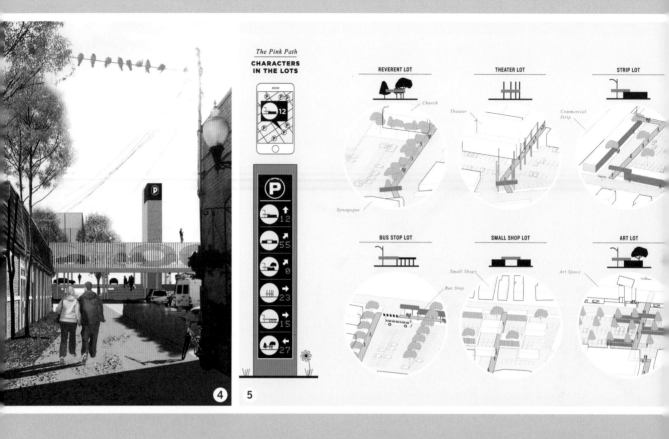

of these tools at peripheral sites along Columbus's ring highway. Zoning was a systematic way to study form.

Recently I've become very interested in the form of suburban building typologies. While it can be somewhat difficult to read the overarching structure of suburban form, one thing that is very legible is the repetitiveness of its different elements. Because the suburbs were constructed so quickly—the elements of the strip mall, public schools and regional malls, for example—they have a very basic and consistent DNA. Currently I'm working with Roberto Diamani at the University of Toronto, looking at the effects of regional malls on their immediate surroundings.

GDA: What representation tools are you using to document and describe and these repetitive suburban forms?

MP: We actually began by drawing the figure ground of the suburbs, looking specifically at regional malls. While this isn't a new way of drawing the city, as the suburbs aren't typically thought of having legible form, we thought it would be interesting to question this assumption. Very quickly we understood that there were latent organizational strategies of the mall and the various buildings that surround them.

Looking at aggregation requires simple drawing techniques. To understand the logics of accumulation, we are making time-lapsed plan drawings that show aggregation over time. One technique of aggregation is what we're calling "crowding," which looks at how various building types group around a mall. For that work we used axonometric drawings to show how different building massings relate to the pancake shape of the mall.

In a way, these research methods relate back to Kevin Lynch. While *Image of the City* is famous for the interviews that engage the constituents of the city, the underlying assertion is that the urbanist's jobs is to make legible that which is not. While the city may be very complex, Lynch sees the role of the urbanist as someone who can tease out the formal clarity embedded within cities. What's fascinating for me is that his own method of analysis really only works in Boston— when he studies more complex cities such as Los Angeles or Jersey City, the method falls apart. I really appreciate Lynch for acknowledging this shortcoming. In doing so, I think he opened the door for others to contribute to research methods.

GDA: What are the ways you're expanding the research methods?

6

MP: I worked on a project with Matthew Allen and Ultan Byrne called *Characters*. With this project we looked at clusters of building types in suburban Toronto and sought to map out repetitive formal parts. The constituent parts of these characters are similar to Lynch's symbology for the city. When assembled in different ways, the characters spell out typologically similar open spaces, but with characteristics unique to each site. There was a desire to make legible these repetitions in the metro area.

GDA: Layering is a theme in your practice. How does layering structure your work?

MP: I think that metro regions today are too complex to proffer any one method of analysis. I am interested in overlaps between different urban practices: negotiating systems and formal analysis to better understand the everyday. When I was in graduate school and immediately after, I took for granted the relevance of form for urbanism. I felt there it was frivolous, inappropriate for engaging ordinary city space. Like many of my colleagues, I became interested in infrastructural systems, and in abstracted diagrammatic methods to represent them. Recently, though, there seems to be a renewed interest in urban form, and an emergent return to more normative methods of representation. Personally, I'm interested in trying to understand the physical space of cities along with their more abstract systems; in using figure grounds, systems diagrams and illustrative methods in parallel. My interest in layering information also drives an interest in layering different methods of observation.

↑ **SUBURBAN FORMS**

Images from projects studying the organization and structure of suburban spaces.

1: Sub Hub. *Michael Piper and Frank Ruchala*

2-3: Characters. *Michael Piper, Matthew Allen and Ultan Byrne*

4-6: The Pink Path. *Michael Piper, Sarah Williams and Ultan Byrne*

PRESENTING TO AN AUDIENCE

PRESENTATIONS

STRUCTURING EVIDENCE

HOW DOES A PRESENTATION INTRODUCE AN IDEA? Step-by-step to build to an inevitable conclusion, or with broader concepts that are broken down into clear details. It all depends on how information is displayed and organized through the presentation.

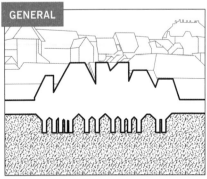

GENERAL

A CONCEPT ABOUT AGGREGATION

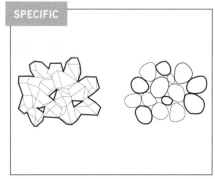

SPECIFIC

EXPLAIN IT IN FURTHER DETAIL

STARTING POINT
Depending on how information is presented, it can be helpful to start with general or specific details, allowing the narrative of the project to unfold. Knowing the audience, too, can help direct which way to organize the presentation.

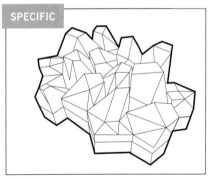

SPECIFIC

BECOME MORE SPECIFIC

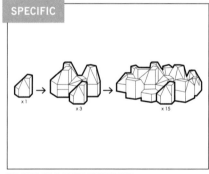

SPECIFIC

BREAK IT DOWN FURTHER

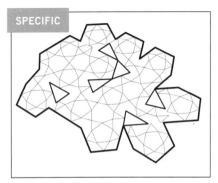

SPECIFIC

SHOW ROOF DETAILS

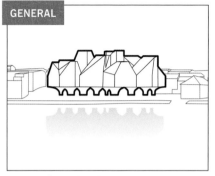

GENERAL

SUPPORT THE ORIGINAL CONCEPT

⊕ SEQUENCE AFFECTS INFORMATION

The same content presented different ways impacts the way information is perceived. Will your work focus on the technical aspects of a project? Or are you more interested in the topological? Presenting and sequencing information impacts the way it is understood.

SPECIFIC

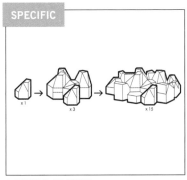

A SINGULAR UNIT

GENERAL

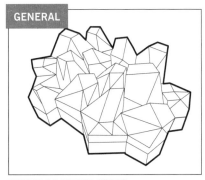

MAKES A LARGER SPACE

GENERAL

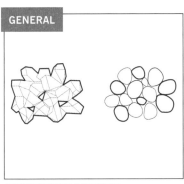

AGGREGATION CONCEPT

GENERAL

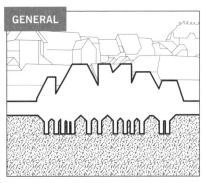

ALSO FOUND IN THE CITY

GENERAL

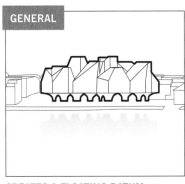

CREATES A FLOATING DATUM

SPECIFIC

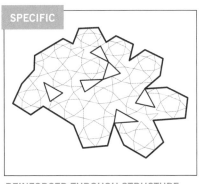

REINFORCED THROUGH STRUCTURE

*Diagrams after Stan
Allen Architect New
Maribor Art Gallery*

NOTES ON:

MAKING AN ARGUMENT

At their very center, presentations are about making arguments. There are many different ways to structure information and position evidence.

DEDUCTIVE REASONING
starts with a general case and deduces specific instances.

SYSTEMIC REASONING
is a way of understanding a whole system. The parts are not just analyzed, but also the relationships between the parts.

COMPARATIVE REASONING
establishes the importance of something by comparing it against something else: the past with the future, for example, or what exists against an ideal.

INDUCTIVE REASONING
draws inferences from observations in order to make generalizations.

DECOMPOSITION
breaks things in question into their component parts, analyzes them to see how they fit together, then draws conclusions about the whole.

COMPACTING MESSAGES

EVERY COMPLEX ARGUMENT HAS SUBSETS OF THEMES. In organizing a presentation slide, consider ways to group information into more managable sections. It is not a practice of separating information as much as reorganizing messages into similar themes.

Too many abbreviations

START

Combined Sewer Overflows (CSOs) in New York City account for about ten percent of the Combined Sewer Overflows (CSOs) in the United States. New York City has 494 (CSO) locations, 13 of which are identified as Tier 1, which are classified as those producing more than 500 million gallons of waste each year. Tier 1 CSOs contribute approximately 50% of the 30 billion annual gallons of Combined Sewage dumped into New York's waterways.

NYC's CSOs

- About ten percent of the Combined Sewer Overflows (CSOs) in the United States are found in the New York system.
- New York City has 494 (CSO) locations.
- Of those, 13 are Tier 1 CSOs, which are those producing more than 500 mgy.
- Tier 1 CSOs contribute approximately 50% of the 30 billion annual gallons of Combined Sewage dumped into New York's waterways

TEXT BLOCK

Presenting dense information can make anyone's eyes quickly glaze over.

No one wants to read your presentation

STARTING POINT

Information is broken into chunks via bullet points. A title centered at the top of the slide orients viewers to the topic.

New York City's Combined Sewer Overflows

- About **ten percent** of the Combined Sewer Overflows (CSOs) in the United States are found in the New York system.
- New York City has **494 (CSO) locations**.
- Of those, **13 are Tier 1 CSOs**, which are those producing more than **500 mgy**.
- Tier 1 CSOs contribute approximately **50% of the 30 billion annual gallons** of Combined Sewage dumped into New York's waterways.

New York City's
Combined Sewer Overflows

- About **ten percent** of the Combined Sewer Overflows (CSOs) in the United States are found in the New York system.
- New York City has **494 (CSO) locations**.
- Of those **13 are Tier 1 CSOs**, which are those producing more than **500 mgy**.
- Tier 1 CSOs contribute approximately **50% of the 30 billion annual gallons** of Combined Sewage dumped into New York's waterways.

INFORMATION HIERARCHIES

Use typography and alignment to craft information:
- **Text weight—bold versus light**
- **Spacing, centering, aligning text**
- **Color to focus attention**

ADDING COLOR

Color should be used to craft information. Be wary of color schemes that serve as decorative highlights.

Is color shaping information? Why are the bullet points green?

OVERVIEW:

NEW YORK CITY'S COMBINED SEWER OVERFLOWS

An unobtrusive line holds the title from the text

- **10 percent** of the United States' Combined Sewer Overflows (CSOs) are located in New York

- New York City has **494** CSOs

- 13 of these produce **50% of the waste**

  Bold text in color helps craft the message

- Each year, **30 billion gallons** of sewage is dumped into New York's waterways

  Lighter text with more space between lines

EDITED

NEW YORK CITY
Combined Sewer Overflow
8pt bold / 8pt light

New York City
COMBINED SEWER OVERFLOW
8pt bold / 7pt light tracking +50

NEW YORK CITY
COMBINED SEWER OVERFLOW
6pt bold –25 tracking / 7pt light

NEW YORK CITY
Combined Sewer Overflow
8pt light +50 / bold –25 tracking

COMBINED SEWER OVERFLOW
Combined Sewer Overflow
7pt bold +25 tracking / 9pt light grey

COMBINED SEWER OVERFLOW
Combined Sewer Overflow
7pt light grey / bold

COMBINED SEWER OVERFLOW
Combined Sewer Overflow
7pt bold grey / 8pt light

COMBINED SEWER OVERFLOW
Combined Sewer Overflow
6pt light / 8pt bold grey

 ALL ONE TYPE

The slides on these pages were made with a single typeface—various sizes, weights, cases, colors and spacing give shape.

COMBINED SEWER OVERFLOW
Combined Sewer Overflow
bold

COMBINED SEWER OVERFLOW
Combined Sewer Overflow
medium

COMBINED SEWER OVERFLOW
Combined Sewer Overflow
light

STRUCTURING COLOR

COLOR IS PERCEIVED IN RELATIONSHIP TO OTHER COLORS. Selecting a color scheme is about balancing the background with selected colors. White backgrounds host most colors without distraction and high contrast.

 MAIN COLOR

Several color palettes can be constructed from a single color.

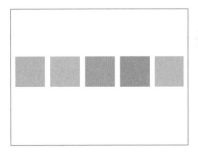 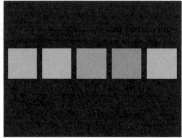 

ANALOGOUS colors on the color wheel are adjacent to one another.

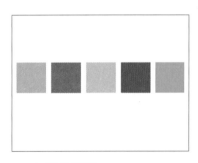 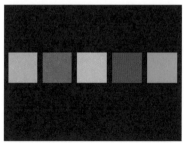 

COMPLEMENTARY colors on the color wheel are opposite one another.

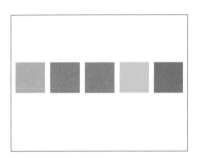 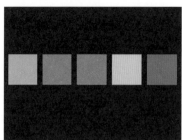 

COMPOUND colors are more earth-toned in nature and contain elements of all the primary hues.

ANALOGOUS	COMPLEMENTARY	COMPOUND

✓ Good contrast

✓ Good contrast

✓ Good contrast

✗ No matter how theoretically sound, colors must work in context

✓ Contrast is OK, but that's a lot of green

✗ Not enough contrast

✗ Close, but not enough contrast

✓ To achieve contrast, the background color is used to find a new complement

✗ Not enough contrast

✓ ✗ This has sufficient contrast, but the atmosphere of placing soft greens against hard black is harsh

✓ ✗ Orange and green are legible but, placed together against a black background, aren't terribly attractive

✓ ✗ Same assessment for the colors green, pink and black

FROM WORDS TO IMAGES

A PRESENTATION IS NOT A DOCUMENT, IT IS A VISUAL TOOL. Presenters should never read from their slides verbatim, but rather use them as a tool for a lecture.

Solid colors are better than gradients

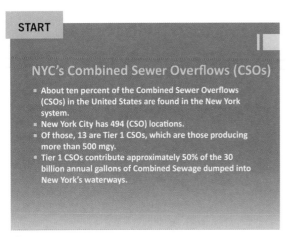

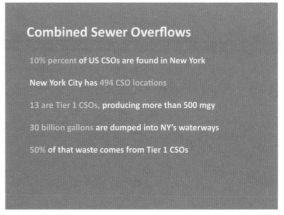

TOO MANY WORDS, DECORATIVE COLOR

Avoid bulleted lists of detailed information. Too many words, especially if they're presented verbatim, produces a dry presentation. Why listen when one can simply read?

BETTER COLOR, STILL TOO MANY WORDS

Rather than used as decoration, color now guides the presentation to highlight key figures. There is still too much text, but now color creates hierarchies of information.

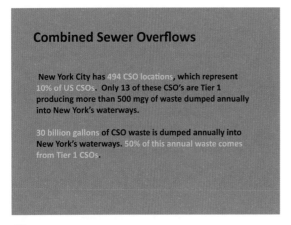

CONTINUE TO REGROUP

As the words are reorganized into better groups, priority information becomes apparent. What are the key messages to convey?

CLARIFY AND EMPHASIZE

Without a lot of extra text and information, it is easy to understand the main point.

↓ THREE-DIMENSIONAL DATA

The same information presented in two bar charts is also presented in this three-dimensional, more picturesque representation of information that begins to approximate architectural volume. when you use 2-D or 3-D.

COMBINED SEWER OVERFLOWS

50% of New York's CSO waste comes from only **13 CSOs**

COMBINED SEWER OVERFLOWS

50% of New York's CSO waste comes from only **13 CSOs**

STAY AWAY FROM CLIP ART

Clip art and other simple illustrations tend to present a serious issue as childish or lighthearted.

AND THE OVERLY LITERAL

An overly accurate or literal photo can easily deter your audience from connecting to your message.

COMBINED SEWER OVERFLOWS

50% of New York's CSO waste comes from only **13 CSOs**

13 CSOs = 50% of the waste

Solid waste never looked so spa-like

QUALITY STOCK IMAGES

High-quality images can emphasize the point without distracting from the intended message.

YOUR OWN PHOTOS

Rather than use an image to illustrate the current problem, reference a design project that projects an optimistic future.

INTERBORO PARTNERS

TOBIAS ARMBORST, DANIEL D'OCA AND GEORGEEN THEODORE, PRINCIPALS / NEW YORK, NY

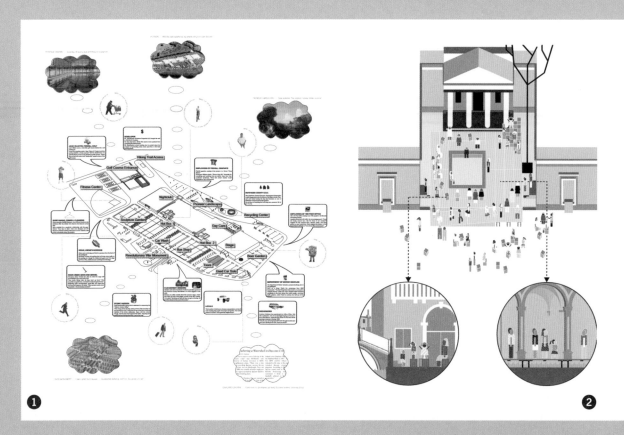

❶   ❷

INTERBORO PARTNERS *is a New York City–based office of architects, urban designers and planners. Partners work together to improve cities with innovative, experimental design ideas. Interboro has won many awards for its innovative projects, including the MoMA PS1 Young Architects Program, the AIA New York Chapter's New Practices Award, and the Architectural League's Emerging Voices and Young Architects Awards.*

GRAPHIC DESIGN FOR ARCHITECTS: How do you recognize the impacts people have on the places they occupy? What kinds of drawings do you make to demonstrate these relationships?

INTERBORO PARTNERS: Our method is to look at existing conditions, to observe what's already there and to understand the community by the different ways space is used and designed. We're deeply interested in what already exists, so we study what places look like, how people use spaces and how they transform them. This forms the basis for how we work.

We like to say we have three roles that stand in for our design methodologies.

When we're studying space as "Detectives," we try to understand what's going on by looking closely, by trying to make sense of what's going on. When we're designing as "Life Coaches," we try to make suggestions about how the site could work better. When we're operating as "Ghost Writers," we try to position these observations by developing narratives to explain how and why a site is designed and occupied.

GDA: Do your drawings change when you're operating in these different ways?

IP: We don't reserve different drawing techniques for different roles because the roles frequently overlap. One of the

things we always try to represent are the conditions that influence a site. These observations help us as we're designing, but they also help people who have a stake in those places see them in a new way. Whenever we act in these different roles, we are taking a stance by visualizing these seemingly forgotten, everyday, common sites in entirely new ways.

GDA: How do your drawings depict these social conditions?

IP: Our first project, *Life with Landbanking,* established our design methodology and also defined the way we developed our drawings. First, we wanted a drawing that

brought in all of the site constituents. Since the project was speculative, we imagined the needs and desires of the different actors on the site. We observed the guy with the driving range, the dry cleaner, the hot dog salesman—people for whom the death of the mall brought a kind of new life. We had to develop a way to bring these people's desires into the project. Bringing other voices into the drawing required a different type of drawing than, say, a final rendering of the finished project. We needed to represent the activities that had already happened, and use this as the basis for how we would project the mall's future. To do this, the *Landbanking* drawing brought in a layer of time—the

↑ **EXPANDING ROLES**

1: In the Meantime: Life with Landbanking, *winning entry to the LA Forum for Architecture's "Dead Malls" Competition*

2, 6: Commonplace, *installation for the 2012 Venice Biennale US Pavilion*

3–5: Holding Pattern, *installation for the 2011 Young Architects Program*

7–8: *2009 International Architecture Biennale Rotterdam*

past, present and future of the mall. For example, the outer ring of the axonometric imagined the future of our design. We were speculating about how our interventions would transform as economic conditions changed. When we were invited by the Walker Art Center to exhibit our proposal for *Landbanking*, we presented the project as a series of projections on a base of the existing mall. Since we were talking about design that would change over time, we wanted the model also to be temporary.

The drawing also brought in people, their interests and personalities. The *Landbanking* project shows the different constituents we observed on the site, demonstrates our design strategies and shows how those elements interact with each other.

GDA: Your drawing for the PS1 Competition had a similar task of showing the extended life of your design proposal.

IP: The PS1 drawing shows moments in the future when our project is being enacted on, engaging with the public and changing. What happens after architecture is constructed? At that stage architecture is based more in time and processes. It interacts with people and sometimes its value changes—when the building is finished, it's not complete but will instead change and adapt over time.

It's interesting to define our role by thinking about what comes *before* we enter the scene and also by what happens *after*. That way of thinking about a design's future requires different types of representation and story telling—such as the cartoon or bubble graphics—to get people's thoughts and feelings into a drawing. It's not just about the building but about how people respond to the work.

GDA: How *do* people respond to your work, both as drawings or built projects?

IP: We believe architecture should be friendly, it should open, it should be something that engages the community in which it's centered. And when architecture becomes open and collaborative, there are some people that say "that's not 'architectural.'" A comment on one of the blogs for the PS1 courtyard project asked "Where's the architecture?"

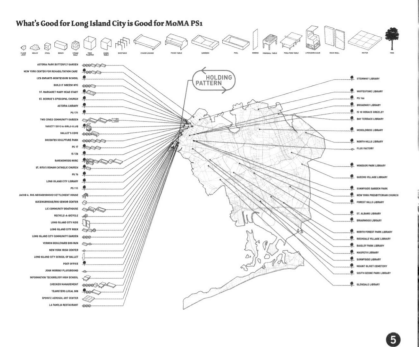

What's Good for Long Island City is Good for MoMA PS1

We don't think architectural drawings need to be communicating to other architects. We should be connected to more people. We use these drawing techniques to engage a broader range of people into the process. We're expanding the role of the architect.

GDA: Would you say that the way you draw the site influences the way you approach the design?

IP: When we drew the courtyard at PS1, we tried using a more conventional architectural drawing, but we shifted it slightly and arranged it in a flattened way. We tried to make this drawing so there was confusion between the spaces in the courtyard. We did this to see those spaces in a new way. In looking back at

the previous entries, everyone has shown the courtyard at a 45 degree angle, which means the courtyard has always been shown in the same way. We realized that view wasn't giving us the entire courtyard, which was funny because no one had ever done anything in this front space. We thought if we could show the space in a new way, we could show how we were using the courtyard in a new way. It was a beautiful moment when we flipped the drawing because now we could see the entire courtyard and see our entire project.

GDA: How do you organize information at different scales and with different modes of representation?

IP: Our proposal for the Rotterdam Biennale was an interesting project

because the organization of the map on the wall is a significant part of how we were designing the relationships between the pieces. In this way the map is similar to our previous axonometrics. We had a collection of communities, conditions and locations and we wanted to show how they related to each other. We didn't want to show a map of the United States because the exhibition space was very long and narrow, and we wanted to fill the corridor. We also didn't want to show the sites in relationship to other sites, or show states against states. We also had a series of case studies and we didn't want to represent them as a serial (Case Study One, Two, etc.). For us, the space between the communities was not important. We wanted to show how they related to each other conceptually than geographically.

Photo by Michelle Wilderom

⑦

We made an imaginary road trip to connect all of these places. The space on the wall isn't a real space, but it's an imagined space that holds these different conditions together. We also had to layer different drawing types together to depict the conditions, changing between plan and elevation. We also used a colored-lens technique to bring more detailed information into the wall graphic.

The second part of the exhibition included *The Arsenal of Inclusion and Exclusion,* which outlines physical and planning techniques that influence settlement. Each "weapon" of inclusion and exclusion is posted as a dictionary entry, A to Z, which is opposite the long map. The exhibition was foundational to how we thought about displaying this work, how to reveal and demonstrate these different types of information.

The visitor experienced these different communities and techniques as they walked through the exhibition. It was a big and very exciting project for us.

GDA: *The Arsenal* presents differently from some of your other projects. Is this because it's primarily text?

IP: We developed this project with Thumb Design who also collaborated with us on *Holding Pattern.* Together we thought of presenting *The Arsenal* as a dictionary, organizing all of the tools alphabetically. Since all of the techniques are weapons that make inclusion or exclusion in communities, we wanted an even rhythm to the presentation. Nothing has more prominence than anything else, which made the entries seem all the more stark and powerful.

We started by crafting five tours through *The Arsenal* since visitors may not want to read everything A to Z. Tour Number One is about understanding why America is so racially segregated. So all of the techniques that enhance segregation are stamped number one. Number Two is about the role of the Fair Housing Act. By giving different slices of information, visitors make their own exhibition books.

This collection is about the arrangement of different elements. How do you exhibit a lot of text? All at once and exaggerated? We used a really big serif typeface to explain the weapons, and also to make it feel more like an encyclopedia, dictionary or library. The exhibition space is made out of an unfolded dictionary and has elements from a domestic library.

Another element that we're interested in is our graphic techniques. In *Holding*

Photo by Noit Zakay

8

Pattern, for example, we were exploring the role of the museum label. So we made them super large and they were used as reserve tags to identify the objects' future owners. We appropriated the museum label and then blew it up and changed its content to become something more accessible. It was the same case at the NAI with our dictionary and library. We're playing with these graphic techniques from other disciplines and tweaking them to make them more accessible and a little bit new. We're interested in representation that comes from outside of architecture. We take pleasure in looking at these other things and transforming them into something new for architecture. We like to use elements that are outside of architecture so people can understand the tools and processes we're engaging. In this way we're also challenging the

authority of the library or the museum and asking these institutions to become part of the community.

GDA: As your practice has grown, the projects become more complex and stakeholders more diverse, how have your drawings evolved?

IP: In practice today there's a race to the bottom. People tend to send their technical drawings out to other places to be rendered, so the value of being able to represent your ideas is decreasing. One of the best things architects can do is to advocate for and communicate their ideas. And having more skills to become inventive with how ideas are demonstrated, that helps our creativity. We use architectural drawings not just to make technical documents or spectacular statements

about material and form, but to advocate for other outcomes. Generally, it becomes more and more important for architects to do work before and after the actual building. You can speculate or advocate for something later or earlier in the process. The traditional architecture documents are somewhat limited in describing the beginnings and ends of architecture. We're interested in how to demonstrate perceptions, observations, feelings that help people become interested in ideas they had not previously considered. How we communicate and advocate those ideas is increasingly important to our practice and the discipline.

BOOKS

PRINTING TECHNOLOGY

↓ HAND-PRINTING PRESS

Type is set, inked and pressed onto paper, producing single sheets at a time (each sheet, or signature, may contain several pages). For each color change, a new plate is inked and pressed onto the same page.

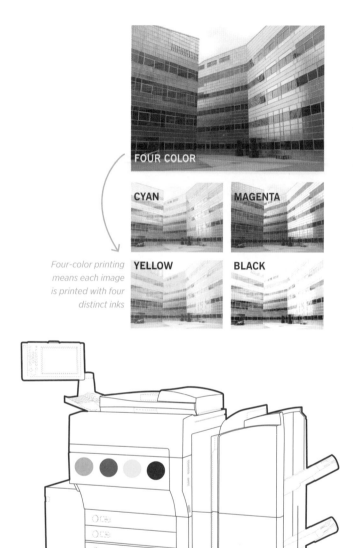

FOUR COLOR

CYAN **MAGENTA**

YELLOW **BLACK**

Four-color printing means each image is printed with four distinct inks

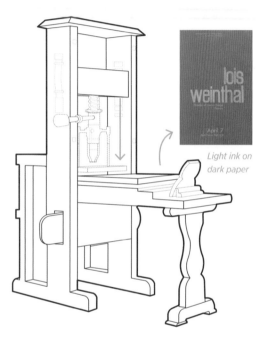

Light ink on dark paper

Gutenberg's sheets were pressed twice—first with black ink then a second pass with red ink

↑ DIGITAL PRINTING

On a four-color press, each image is printed with a separate layer of ink which builds into a composite. This is why you need to convert your RGB images to CMYK when prepping files for press production.

To print the magazine with fluorescent inks, but to stay within a four-color budget, typical inks were swapped with custom Pantone colors

RUN 1: 802U + BLACK

RUN 2: 804U + BLACK

| 802U | 804U | 805U | 801U | | BLACK | VARNISH |

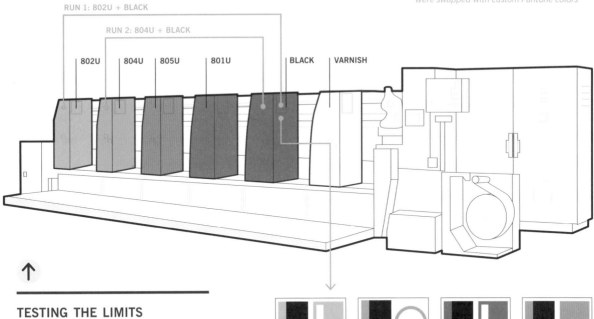

↑

TESTING THE LIMITS

Knowing how printing technology works allows the designer to engage the printing process. Meeting with subcontractors and discussing the potentials allows for better professional collaborations.

A series of 2-color signatures are printed and assembled together to create a "4-color" magazine

BOOK ERGONOMICS

BOOKS HAVE A PHYSICAL PRESENCE. As they are held in the hand and experienced with our eyes, they relate to the human body. Because books are far more dense and physical than portfolios, designing a book's physical presence—mass, weight and structure—is part of designing a book's message. Books sequence information, but they also have a permanence—they mobilize performance and make physical architectural ideas.

A5
5.833" x 8.24"

US TRADE
6" x 9"

 ## SMALL BOOKS

Since small books fit into the hand and are meant to be enjoyed by one person at a time, they are personal and have an intimacy. One's engagement with small books is more akin to trade paperbacks—meant to be seen by the individual, not a group, and pored over in an intimate way. Small books are personal.

US TRADE
6" x 9"
15.24cm x
22.86cm

A5
5.833" x 8.24"
14.817cm x
20.99cm

ROYAL
6.139" x 9.21"
15.593cm x
23.389cm

POCKET
4.25" x 6.875"
10.795cm x
17.463cm

 ## STANDARD BOOKS

Standard book sizes have a different physical quality than small books. Their mass and weight require two hands to hold the object rather than just one. When opened, the page spread takes on a larger territory.

US LETTER
8.5" x 11"
21.59cm x
27.94cm

A4
8.264" x 11.694"
20.99cm x
29.70cm

CROWN QUARTO
7.444" x 9.681"
18.91cm x
24.589cm

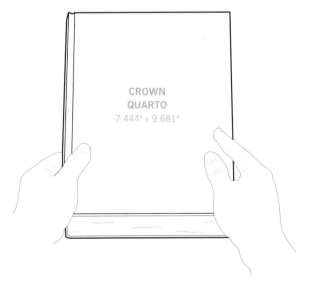

CROWN
QUARTO
7.444" x 9.681"

↓ OPEN VERSUS CLOSED

When opened, books have a very different quality. The territory of the page set-up dramatically changes. A landscape page has a much different proportion than a spread of two landscape pages.

LANDSCAPE
7" x 9"

OPENED LANDSCAPE
7" x 18"

18"

7"

→ ONE HAND OR TWO

Book sizes relate to the scale of the body and how it fits into your hand, how far it is held from your face and how much content, images and text occupy the page.

Larger gutter

Larger margins

When setting up the page margins and gutters, consider how the book will be held

↓

NOTES ON:

BINDINGS FOR BOOKS

Because books are longer, have more pages and don't need to quickly disseminate a lot of visual information in just a few pages, they can afford different bindings than portfolios.

HARD COVERS

Case-wrapped books provide a solid shell for the interior pages. Their durability allows the book to open without cracking the spine.

SOFT COVERS

Paperback books are perfect bound, so as a result don't lie flat when opened. Due to their physical limits, the interior margin needs to be considered when designing the book. If designing a small, perfect-bound book, the margin is going to take on a different territory than a larger perfect-bound book.

SEWN BINDINGS

Sewn bindings are the most durable type and are when the book block is actually sewn with thread before binding. Sewing the book block ensures the binding doesn't crack, which can happen on larger glue-bound books or books that are opened and closed hundreds of times.

PACING AND SEQUENCE

DIFFERENT TYPES OF PAGES HOLD DIFFERENT TYPES OF INFORMATION.

Page types coordinate a book's pacing by varying the way content is displayed,
giving a book hierarchy and structure.

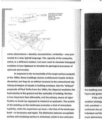

INTRO PHOTO ESSAY

Black and white images on toned paper announce each new section. Small captions annotate the images, giving another layer of interpretation.

INTRO CONTEXT ESSAY

Essay contextualizes the proceeding visual essay. Toned paper is a slightly lighter in color than the visual essay. Large-sized sans serif text is set in one column.

EXAMPLE PROJECTS

Starts with an introductory photo that spans a two-page spread. Large and medium-sized photos are used. Two columns of serif body text describe the projects.

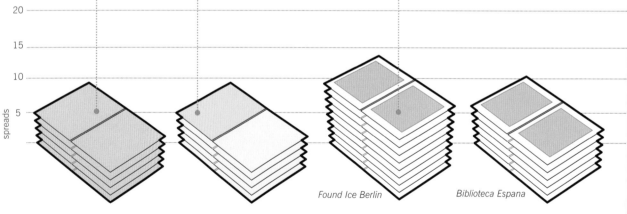

Found Ice Berlin

Biblioteca Espana

SECTION INTRODUCTION		PROJECTS		
Form Photos	Form Essay	Found Ice Berlin	Biblioteca Espana	Museo Territorio

64   84

Essay pages are filled with text and contain smaller images, while gallery spreads have larger images and fewer words

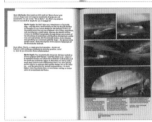

INTERVIEW

Dialogue between participants. A single column of serif body text is indented to describe the dialogue. A selection of smaller black and white images illustrate the discussion.

ESSAY

Critical and historic overview to the section topic. Serif body text is set in a single column. Larger black and white images

CONCLUDING PROJECT

Deep inquiry into focused project. Blue pages with darker blue type, full-bleed images.

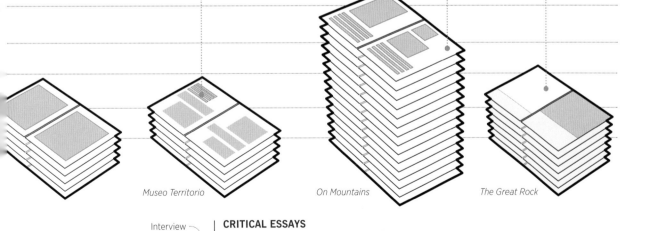

Museo Territorio   *On Mountains*   *The Great Rock*

Interview   **CRITICAL ESSAYS**

On Mountains   *The Great Rock*

124   132   136   167   179

Stan Allen and Mark McQuade. *Landform Building: Architecture's New Terrain.* (Baden: Lars Muller, 2011)

PAGE GRIDS

ONE GRID SYSTEM CAN ORGANIZE MANY DIFFERENT TYPES OF CONTENT. A
12-column grid can accommodate two, three, four and six page divisions as well as organize
a variety of image and text sizes. Flexible grid systems can adapt to many circumstances.

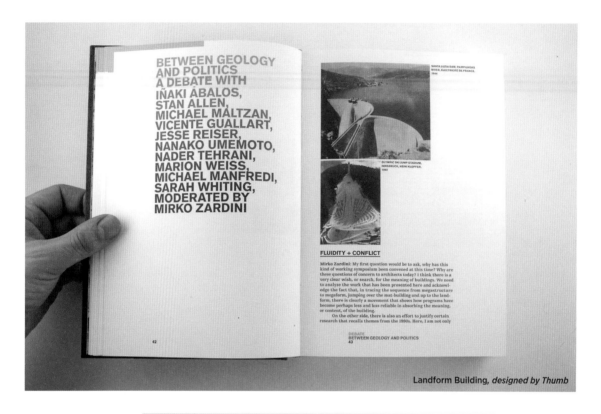

*Landform Building, **designed by Thumb***

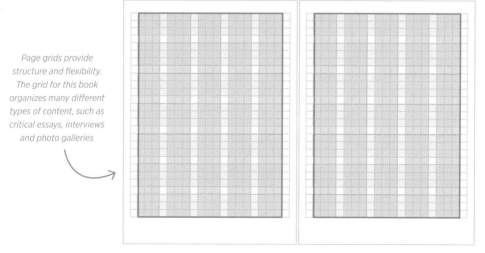

*Page grids provide
structure and flexibility.
The grid for this book
organizes many different
types of content, such as
critical essays, interviews
and photo galleries*

Prototypical grid for Landform Building *book*

ENDLESS VARIATION

Books have to manage a lot of different types of content. In this book, scholarly articles, photo galleries, contextualizing essays and large images are all managed with the same grid system, giving a cohesive presentation to a variety of information.

Essay with large images

Full-bleed image with caption

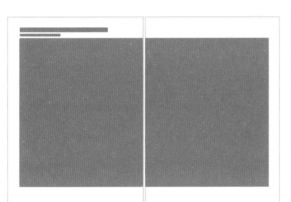

Large photo with title

Smaller images, large text

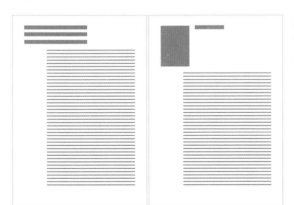

Essay – mostly text

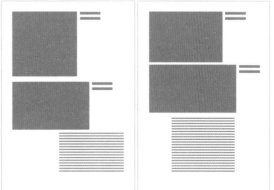

Images with text

STRUCTURING THE PAGE

SEVERAL METHODS CAN ESTABLISH THE RELATIONSHIPS between page edge and text. How you set up the logic of page margins can be systematic, such as some of the classical proportional systems suggested, or more intuitive, based on your own sense of balance.

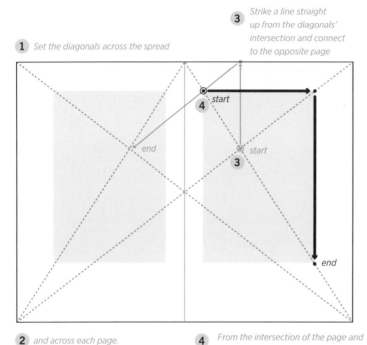

3 *Strike a line straight up from the diagonals' intersection and connect to the opposite page*

1 *Set the diagonals across the spread*

start

4

end

start

3

end

2 *and across each page.*

4 *From the intersection of the page and spread diagonals, draw a line across until it hits the spread diagonal.*

J. A. VAN DE GRAAF CANON

This classic text-block-to-page-size proportioning system is less relevant to contemporary practice, but recognizing its origins allows for reinvention. After studying books designed between 1450 and 1500, Van de Graaf discovered a consistency in how the text block was placed in relationship to the page size. This diagram results in the top left corner and the inside margin always being 1/9th from the top and the inside margin, producing a consistently balanced text block.

Jan Tschichold refers to this system as a "method to produce the perfect book"

THE GOLDEN RATIO

This proportional system of squares and rectangles is based on the Fibonacci sequence, and can be found in nature, Western art and architecture (Le Corbusier's *Villa Stein*, for example or *The Mona Lisa*). A distinctive feature of this shape is that when a square section is removed, the remainder is another golden rectangle; that is, with the same aspect ratio as the first. Hence a : b = b : (a+b).

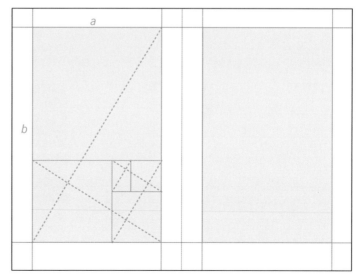

a

b

$a : b = b : (a+b)$

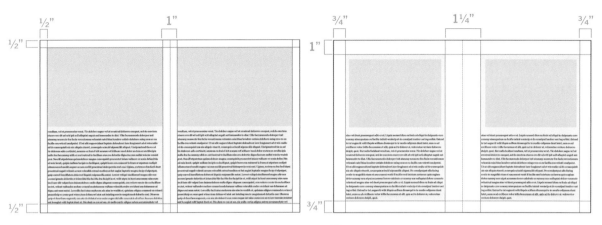

½"   1"

½"

½"

¾"   1¼"   ¾"

1"

¾"

✗ DEFAULT MARGINS

When placing text on a page, avoid the default setting of an even margin around the perimeter of each page edge. Pages should be thought about as spreads, and as physical devices collected into a book. Gutters, edges, page titles and headers influence the placement of text.

✓ DESIGNED MARGINS

A wider gutter allows for pages to hinge in the center. Margins of different widths at the top of the page versus the bottom allow for headers and footers.

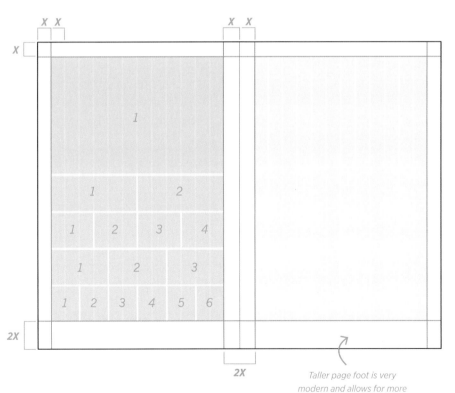

X X   X X

X

2X

2X

12-COLUMN GRID

The simple 12-column grid allows for many subdivisions. It can be easily broken into two, three, four or six subdivisions. Margins are proportional to the interior grid, and can even be incorporated into the overall page structure. This 12-columnn grid allows for maxiumum flexibility, easily combining images and text.

Taller page foot is very modern and allows for more room for page numbers, book titles and navigation

SETTING TYPE

TEXT IS A SYSTEM, NOT AN OBJECT. As a result, the rules of alignment, spacing and proportion are dynamic in order to respond to the ever-changing spaces produced by text.

→ STEP ONE

Text needs to be designed, not just automatically placed using document default settings.

- **Type size is too large**
- **Leading is too solid**
- **Double-justified paragraph creates rivers in the text body**
- **Nominal weight difference between title and body text**

⊗ **HARBORPORT**

Double justification creates rivers of space in paragraphs

Harborport links New York's water management systems with transportation networks at several scales of infrastructure and connectivity. First, the proposal seeks to mitigate combined sewer overflow (CSO) pollution with new subway and ferry connections. The 2014 Clean Tech Expo serves as the public platform for this new investment in infrastructure and water health. Following the Expo, facilities are expanded through collection of river dredge materials toward the construction of a new airport to serve the metro area.

→ CHANGING SCALE

- **Leading is still too solid**
- **Right paragraph rag is choppy**
- **Line length is too long**
- **Avoid widows (single words on a single line)**

⊗ **HARBORPORT**

Choppy rag

Harborport links New York's water management systems with transportation networks at several scales of infrastructure and connectivity. First, the proposal seeks to mitigate combined sewer overflow (CSO) pollution with new subway and ferry connections. The 2014 Clean Tech Expo serves as the public platform for this new investment in infrastructure and water health. Following the Expo, facilities are expanded through collection of river dredge materials toward the construction of a new airport to serve the metro area.

Watch out for orphans

→ TYPES OF TYPE

Perfect!

- **Type size is slightly decreased**
- **Leading is increased**
- **Ironically, as type gets smaller, leading often gets larger**

✓ **HARBORPORT**

Keep line length to eight to ten words per line

Harborport links New York's water management systems with transportation networks at several scales of infrastructure and connectivity. First, the proposal seeks to mitigate combined sewer overflow (CSO) pollution with new subway and ferry connections. The 2014 Clean Tech Expo serves as the public platform for this new investment in infrastructure and water health. Following the Expo, facilities are expanded through collection of river dredge materials toward the construction of a new airport to serve the metro area.

WIDOWS AND ORPHANS

Avoid leaving single lines of text (orphans) or single words (widows) on lines by themselves.

 Harborport links New York's water management systems with transportation networks at several scales of infrastructure and connectivity. *Watch out for orphans*

Eliminate orphans by either changing the length of the type box.

Original length

✓ Harborport links New York's water management systems with transportation networks at several scales of infrastructure and connectivity.

Or adjusting the overall tracking to sneak another word onto the line.

✓ Harborport links New York's water management systems with transportation networks at several scales of infrastructure and connectivity.

Increasing tracking pushes "and" to the next line

Don't leave single lines of text on their own paragraph line.

Avoid widows

 Harborport links New York's water management systems with transportation networks at several scales of infrastructure and connectivity. First, the proposal seeks to mitigate combined sewer overflow (CSO) pollution with new  subway and ferry connections. The 2014 Clean Tech Expo serves as the public platform for this new investment in infrastructure and water health. Following the Expo, facilities are expanded

Adjust the text box, gutter width and / or tracking to help align text.

✓ Harborport links New York's water management systems with transportation networks at several scales of infrastructure and connectivity. First, the proposal seeks to mitigate combined sewer overflow (CSO) pollution with new subway and ferry connections. The 2014 Clean Tech Expo serves as the public platform for this new investment in infrastructure and water health. Following the Expo, facilities are expanded through collection of river dredge materials toward the construction of a new airport to serve the metro area.

NOTES ON:

DASH TYPES

HYPHENS connect a sequence of numbers, such as a phone number.

614-555-1234

EN DASHES are longer than regular dashes (the length of the letter "n") and are used several ways:

- **A range of values** with clearly defined limits.

    From 11:00am–1:00pm
    For ages 3–5

- **To contrast values** or illustrate a relationship.

    Smoot–Hawley Tariff
    Boston beat New York 22–0

- **For compound attributives** in which one or both elements is itself a compound.

    The ex–prime minister
    Pritzker Prize–winning building

EM DASHES are the length of an "m" character and are frequently used mid-sentence to demarcate a break of thought or interruption.

    She was suddenly in a position to call those associates—and invite them to apply to her for jobs.

- **An en dash surrounded by spaces** achieves the same effect as an em dash with no spaces. However, some feel this option is typographically less disruptive.

    She was suddenly in a position to call those associates – and invite them to apply to her for jobs.

POINT SIZE, LEADING AND MEASURE

POINT SIZE, LEADING AND MEASURE contribute to the overall tone and density of how words appear on the page. Slight adjustments to these relationships can dramatically change how type appears.

LEADING

When fonts are set manually, strips of lead are added between lines of type to give them added space. The term "leading," the amount of space between text lines, comes from the strips of lead used to create space in the composing stick.

Leading

Slug

Metal type

A composing stick assembles pieces of metal type

POINT SIZE IS RELATIVE

10 points in one typeface can be relative to 9 points in another. Pick a type size that looks right to you rather than rely on a typical size. Need more help? Compare a *printed* test sample of your text to the size, leading and color of type used in a magazine article.

Harborport links New York's water management systems

Chronicle, Roman, 9 pt

Harborport links New York's water management systems

Garamond, Regular, 10 pt

KERNING AND TRACKING

Kerning adjusts the spacing between individual letters to achieve a more legible, visually pleasing result. Kerning adjusts the space between individual letter forms, while tracking adjusts spacing uniformly over a range of characters.

Slabs align *Slabs overlap*

Av Av

No kerning *Kerning*

Avery Library
No kerning

Avery Library
Kerning

Tracking variations

Avery Library's collection in architecture literature is among the largest in the world.

0

Avery Library's collection in architecture literature is among the largest in the world.

-25

Avery Library's collection in architecture literature is among the largest in the world.

+20

SMALL ADJUSTMENTS

Slight changes between point size and leading can dramatically impact paragraph "color," the appearance of type's texture on the page.

---

8 point / 12 leading   *Lines read as a paragraph*

Harborport links New York's water management systems with transportation networks at several scales of infrastructure and connectivity. First, the proposal seeks to mitigate combined sewer overflow (CSO) pollution with new subway and ferry connections. The 2014 Clean Tech Expo serves as the public platform for this new investment in infrastructure and water health. Following the Expo, facilities are expanded through collection of river dredge materials toward the construction of a new airport to serve the metro area.

8 point / 11 leading

Harborport links New York's water management systems with transportation networks at several scales of infrastructure and connectivity. First, the proposal seeks to mitigate combined sewer overflow (CSO) pollution with new subway and ferry connections. The 2014 Clean Tech Expo serves as the public platform for this new investment in infrastructure and water health. Following the Expo, facilities are expanded through collection of river dredge materials toward the construction of a new airport to serve the metro area.

---

8 point / 14 leading   *Too much space—lines no longer read as a paragraph*

Harborport links New York's water management systems with transportation networks at several scales of infrastructure and connectivity. First, the proposal seeks to mitigate combined sewer overflow (CSO) pollution with new subway and ferry connections. The 2014 Clean Tech Expo serves as the public platform for this new investment in infrastructure and water health. Following the Expo, facilities are expanded through collection of river dredge materials toward the construction of a new airport to serve the metro area.

9 point / 11 leading

Harborport links New York's water management systems with transportation networks at several scales of infrastructure and connectivity. First, the proposal seeks to mitigate combined sewer overflow (CSO) pollution with new subway and ferry connections. The 2014 Clean Tech Expo serves as the public platform for this new investment in infrastructure and water health. Following the Expo, facilities are expanded through collection of river dredge materials toward the construction of a new airport to serve the metro area.

---

10 point / 14 leading

Harborport links New York's water management systems with transportation networks at several scales of infrastructure and connectivity. First, the proposal seeks to mitigate combined sewer overflow (CSO) pollution with new subway and ferry connections. The 2014 Clean Tech Expo serves as the public platform for this new investment in infrastructure and water health. Following the Expo, facilities are expanded through collection of river dredge materials toward the construction of a new airport to serve the metro area.

10 point / 9 leading

Harborport links New York's water management systems with transportation networks at several scales of infrastructure and connectivity. First, the proposal seeks to mitigate combined sewer overflow (CSO) pollution with new subway and ferry connections. The 2014 Clean Tech Expo serves as the public platform for this new investment in infrastructure and water health. Following the Expo, facilities are expanded through collection of river dredge materials toward the construction of a new airport to serve the metro area.

Text is the same point size, but looks very different depending on the leading

THUMB

LUKE BULMAN, FOUNDER AND DIRECTOR / NEW YORK, NY

Expanded Mies

LUKE BULMAN *is founder and director of Thumb, a Brooklyn-based graphic design office that was organized in 2007 by partners Luke Bulman and Jessica Young. Thumb works on public, private and self-initiated projects, usually in the areas of architecture, art, design and culture. The projects featured on these spreads are part of courses taught at the Yale School of Architecture.*

GRAPHIC DESIGN FOR ARCHITECTS: You design books primarily, and many for architects. How has your architectural education in architecture helped you with your current work?

LUKE BULMAN: One of the ways I've approached graphic design is through images. Most of the graphic designers I know have been trained to think about words, a structuralist approach to typography. I've never approached graphic design this way, or learning about architecture in this way. For me, it's about images: looking at images of architecture, paintings, photographs, etc.

The image is the way I frame an argument. I've always thought about the image as the basis of graphic design. That is the way I've linked to architecture.

GDA: In your practice, how do images organize books?

LB: We did a book about David Adjaye's work including some of the studios he taught at Princeton. Different artists were invited to contribute. The book is divided into different pieces—Adjaye's work, work by the invited artists, essays, texts by the artists, parts of conversations, further essays, student works.

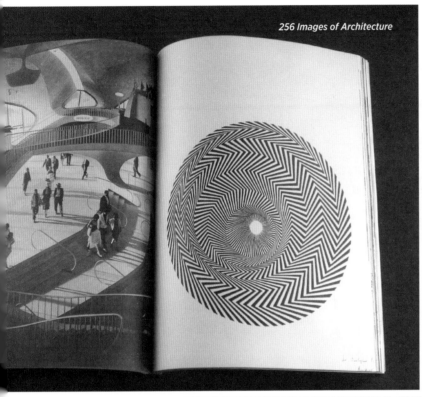

256 Images of Architecture

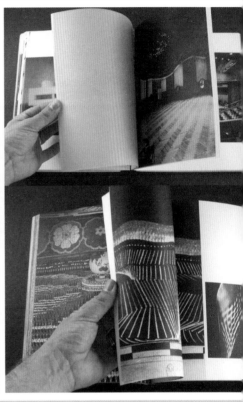

The book forms a repetition. In between each structure are image sets showing the interaction between art and architecture.

Everyone in this book is arguing for something more integrated, where art and architecture become blurred. The blurring of that intellectual line gives a way to think about blurring the lines of the structure of the book. This book has different types of content, which is set in different scales of type, is assembled with different types of paper—some more like newsprint, others shinier and in full color—the images are placed in different ways depending on the types of conversations. These choices give an open structure to the book. The structure is not as vibrant or casual as *S,M,L,XL*, but there's an open figure to it.

GDA: Open figure is a highly architectural term. It strikes me that you speak about books with other architectural terms— structure, flow, figure, for example.

LB: It's a way of talking about the nature of the content, and that by extension I'm always looking for a way to connect the content to the book to its design. I want to leave the structure open enough, not resolved enough, so there are places for people to find something in the book. The difference between watching a New Wave film versus a Hollywood film, for example, is that not everything is explained. I try to make productive frictions between things. I try to make things so much themselves that, when they're placed next to something different or unexpected, the reader has to resolve those differences. The book is deploying things in time, not just spatially, so it's a matter of how closely you time those differences for the reader. Book design is about you handle the space, but it is how you design the time between spreads that produces meaning.

16,392 Images That Matter to Architecture

This exhibition at the 2013 New York Art Book Fair was funded by Elise Jaffe and Jeffrey Brown with support from Yale School of Architecture

GDA: How is your work spatial?

LB: I think of my work as very very 2D and 4D, and not much 3D at all. There are some aspects of the physical book object that I think about as 3D, but not really. This isn't where my work is creative. I think about the deployment of the spreads, I don't really think about how they compile to make a book form.

GDA: How do books contribute to your understanding of architecture?

LB: I've been teaching a class on books and architecture at Yale for five years. One of the projects in the seminar is called 256. It asks students to gather together 256 images that matter to architecture. Everybody has to decide for themselves what those images are—it is a research project is research to figure out what

matters to architecture. Once you have these images, how do you structure and sequence them so they have meaning? The projects become a psychic register of architecture subconsciousness.

I've been obsessed with this book, *Mies van der Rohe* by Werner Blaser. He did several books on Mies, he was from Basel, he worked in Mies's office and did a book when he was there and a whole bunch of other books just documenting the work. It's a super simple book, just documenting the work. There's nothing graphically tricky going on here, it just presents the work. There are a few images that have a handful of people in them, but for the most part the book is just images of buildings. It's sterile, simple, there's no noise—almost pure signal.

This book is simultaneously interesting to me but also dead. There's nothing animating it, there's no life in this book,

compared to *S,M,L,XL*, which figures really strongly in that depiction of life. You have pictures of men's underwear, artwork, dialogue, cartoons, different types of histories of materials and the lexicon. It describes the world and how the practice fits into the world. These connections are what make it enduring—it has an openness.

That's the type of book I'm trying to do. For the seminar at Yale, I proposed we take the Mies book, crack it open and let it drift. We reproduced the Mies book on grey paper and everyone in the seminar contributed sections to the book printed on yellow paper. We tried to bring the material up to date. In between the invention of the TV dinner, the beginning of Burger King, we open the material up to other things that were happening at the same time. It tests the idea Mies put forward—that architecture reflects the time. Is Mies's work an expression of the time he worked in?

GDA: The design of the book is a way to mark changing cultural contexts.

LB: That's one of the things that's really missing right now—context for ideas. No one seems to take that very seriously right now. I participate in a lot of architecture portfolio workshops and I don't see much effort towards producing documentation or proof of concepts. I'm finding that, as we move further into digitization, we are demonstrating technological ability more than conceptual documents. People are not thinking about communication issues as much as they used to.

GDA: Why do you think there is that shift away from communication? What is being discussed instead?

LB: I think there's a switch in the modality of working for architects. BIM software

or any kind of programming environment shifts the location of where the discourse happens. Currently in architecture reviews, students will likely pin up their Grasshopper diagrams which become the documents used to discuss the relative competency of the work. There's less output towards traditional modes of representation and increasingly towards the tectonic of the functioning diagram as proof of concept.

GDA: Increased technological specification has impacted communication—how can architects reclaim presentation techniques?

LB: We've relied on the simultaneous procession through our work for so long —put everything up on the wall and then walk the jury through the work. Now we make presentations through slides that emphasize a temporal procession through the work. The thing we lose in

the slide-type presentation is the big view, the extent of what to look at. This is an important concept, to know the outer edges of the idea and to talk through details that support the concepts. We need to engage with the rhetoric of presentation, with modes of organizing information.

GDA: You're advocating for structure.

LB: It's about understanding the underlying structure of how we organize things. We organize things by scale, typologies, etc. There's an art to these discussions. It's not about software— that's only a tool to achieve the larger goal. We have to take modes of rhetoric and deploy them with new technologies. It is not about describing the design process but about finding ways to capture peoples' imaginations.

DIAGRAMS

THESE ARE THE SHAPES

SOME DIAGRAMS DESCRIBE THE FORM OF ARCHITECTURE, either abstractly or directly, by emphasizing a building's figural characteristics. These diagrams explain the geometric qualities of a building, showing how the architect composed the building's figures, openings and thresholds. "Form diagrams" are useful for helping in understanding geometric and spatial relationships between building components.

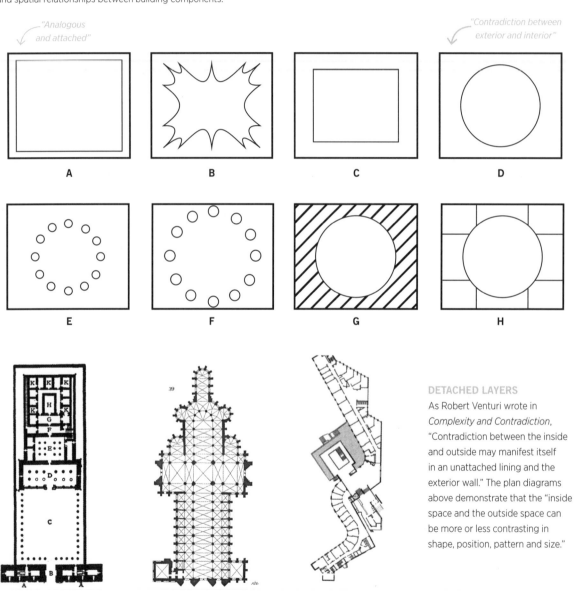

"Analogous and attached"

"Contradiction between exterior and interior"

A   B   C   D

E   F   G   H

Temple of Horus, Edufu, Egypt
"Detached"

Rouen Cathedral, France
"Semi-detached"

Aalto. Baker House, USA
"Detached from front to back"

DETACHED LAYERS

As Robert Venturi wrote in *Complexity and Contradiction*, "Contradiction between the inside and outside may manifest itself in an unattached lining and the exterior wall." The plan diagrams above demonstrate that the "inside space and the outside space can be more or less contrasting in shape, position, pattern and size."

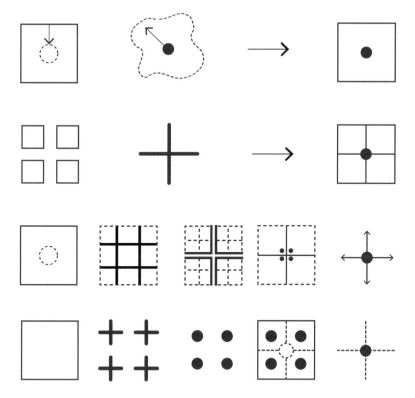

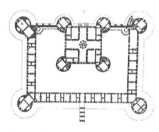

Plan of Chateau de Chambord

INSIDE / OUTSIDE

Doug Graf's essay "Diagrams" establishes the possibility of "knowing architecture" through a dialogue of "object and type, types and typologies." These plan diagrams of Chambord, for example, explore the formal and spatial relationships of the perimeter to the center, the parts to the whole, unity and closure. As the diagrams suggest, there are many ways to understand the forms, relationships and shapes that compose a building.

Doug Graf's investigations of Chambord's perimeter-to-center, part-to-whole relationships

SIMILAR SHAPES

Even though the Venturi House and the Temple of Uffizi appear very different, their formal diagrams are similar. As Graf writes, "The recurring theme... suggest the usefulness of a diagrammatic model that displays its categorizing process."

"Presence–absence, barrier–passage, opposites–equals"

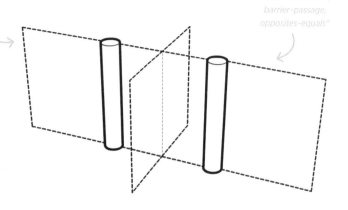

HOW I GOT TO THE SHAPES

DIAGRAMMING THE PROCESS OF GENERATING ARCHITECTURE, versus unearthing the relationships between elements, positions the diagram as a tool for formal decision making. These diagrams offer insight into how the architect has made decisions about a building's form. Sometimes esoteric (Peter Eisenman), other times more straight forward (Bjarke Ingles Group), "step-by-step diagrams" make it is easy to read the architect's form-making process.

Thick, thin and dashed lines help diagrams read

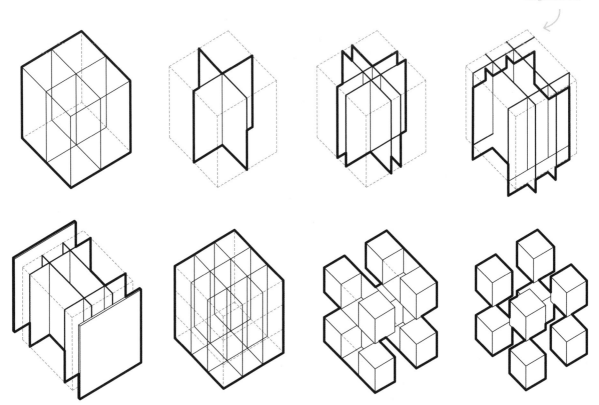

Diagrams after Eisenman House Studies

REPETITION

As Eisenman writes, "The diagram is not only an explanation... but it also acts as an intermediary in the process of generating real space and time." These rigorous diagrams index the architect's inquiry into the formal potential of a cube, layering lines and edges to explore the potential architecture of the final form of the building.

THINKING IN LAYERS

Processing volumes through line weight, shading and color help explain the formal operations.

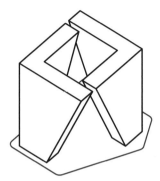

Exterior line weight is thicker than interior

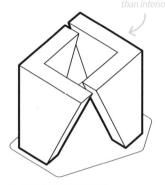

1. OUT OF THE BOX
Straight out of the modeling program, the axon has only one line weight. It is flat and dimensionless.

2. ADD LINE WEIGHT
A simple black-and-white axon with clear line weights help give dimension and space.

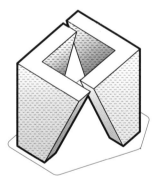

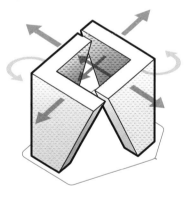

3. ADD HATCHING
A light gradient or texture hatch further emphasizes the volume.

*Diagrams after
Bjarke Ingles Group*

4. ADD ARROWS, TEXT AND COLOR
Graphic elements can help describe movement and other transformations.

NOTES ON:

ACTIVE ARROWS

Like typefaces, arrow styles communicate different intentions. Each computer program has a different language of arrows. If the arrow is wide and flat or thin and delicate, these give tone and intention to a drawing.

SIMPLE WIDE

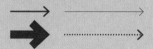

Flat, graphic and without any nuance, the simple wide arrow has different weights and postures depending on line weight and texture.

CURVED / BARBED

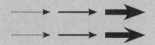

Curves and barbs have more nuance and shape, communicating delicate elegance.

SIMPLE AND SOLID

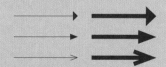

Some stroke weights are better suited to certain types of arrow head. A delicate stroke can look off-centered, or perfectly balanced, with a particular arrow head.

HOW THE PIECES RELATE

DIAGRAMS CAN REVEAL RELATIONSHIPS BETWEEN COMPONENTS. Pulling apart
a large building, landscape or other project shows how different elements configure with
one another. These diagrams emphasize the idea of how the shapes relate, depicting how
organizational strategies relate to the whole.

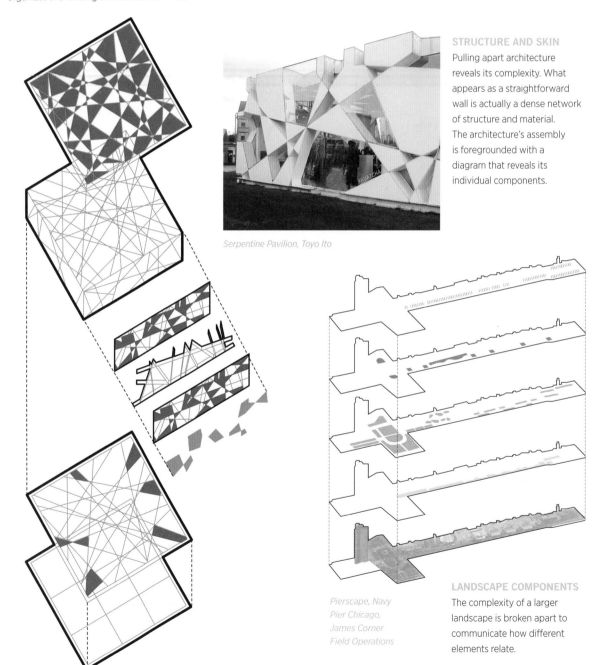

STRUCTURE AND SKIN
Pulling apart architecture
reveals its complexity. What
appears as a straightforward
wall is actually a dense network
of structure and material.
The architecture's assembly
is foregrounded with a
diagram that reveals its
individual components.

Serpentine Pavilion, Toyo Ito

LANDSCAPE COMPONENTS
The complexity of a larger
landscape is broken apart to
communicate how different
elements relate.

*Pierscape, Navy
Pier Chicago,
James Corner
Field Operations*

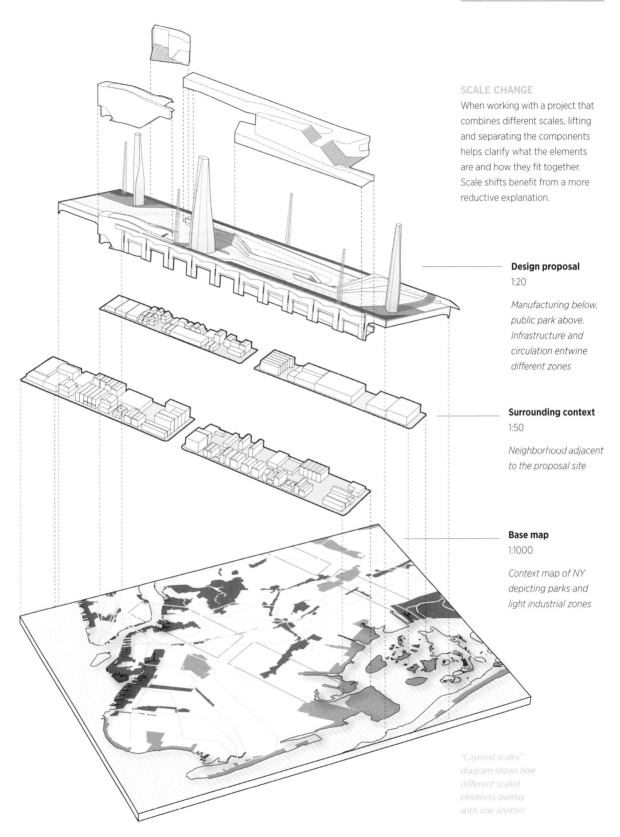

SCALE CHANGE

When working with a project that combines different scales, lifting and separating the components helps clarify what the elements are and how they fit together. Scale shifts benefit from a more reductive explanation.

Design proposal
1:20

Manufacturing below, public park above. Infrastructure and circulation entwine different zones

Surrounding context
1:50

Neighborhood adjacent to the proposal site

Base map
1:1000

Context map of NY depicting parks and light industrial zones

"Layered scales" diagram shows how different scaled elements overlay with one another

PHENOMENOLOGICAL DIAGRAMS

COMPLEXITY CAN OFTEN BE EXPERIENCED, RATHER THAN SEEN. Recognizing the effects and qualities of a space, its tension, compression or movement requires a different set of diagrams to explain their effects. The "phenomenological diagram" helps explain architecture's spatial effects.

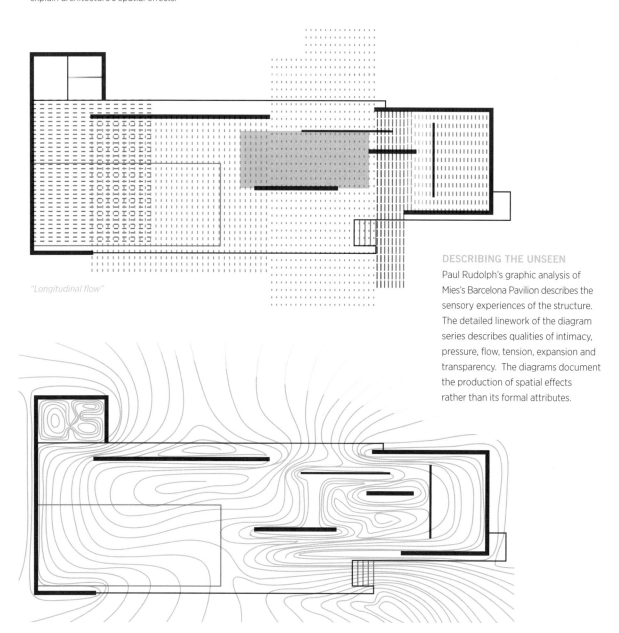

"Longitudinal flow"

DESCRIBING THE UNSEEN

Paul Rudolph's graphic analysis of Mies's Barcelona Pavilion describes the sensory experiences of the structure. The detailed linework of the diagram series describes qualities of intimacy, pressure, flow, tension, expansion and transparency. The diagrams document the production of spatial effects rather than its formal attributes.

"Density flowing space"

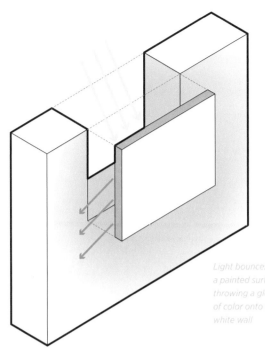

LIGHTING EFFECTS

This diagram of Steven Holl's DeShaw office building demonstrates the atmospheric effects of light reflecting off colored surfaces.

Light bounces off a painted surface, throwing a glow of color onto the white wall

"Positing the perpetual interaction of moving, evolving systems: one invisible (the diagram) and one visible (the real). The primary phenomena studied by the new sciences are actually visible to, or intuitable by, a living observer, but not to a non-living one, say to a camera or a measuring device."

—Sanford Kwinter

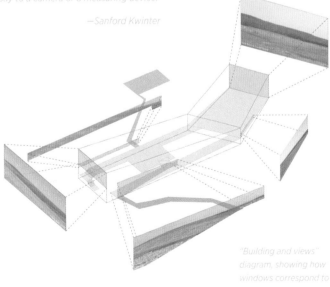

"Building and views" diagram, showing how windows correspond to landscape conditions

NOTES ON:

SOFT FADES

When describing ephemeral effects such as light, wind, pressure and movement, diagrams will employ a different set of graphic techniques that emphasize these qualities.

GRADIENTS

Moving from darkness to light, or density to transparency, the gradient blur is a useful tool to communicate feelings of motion.

STROKE GRADIENTS

If demonstrating movement from one area to another, stroke gradients can reinforce a sense of motion and action.

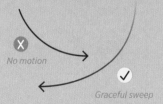

X *No motion*

✓ *Graceful sweep*

FINE LINES, DASHES AND DOTS

Delicate relationships between cause and effect can be communicated with fine lines, dots and dashes. Combined with arrows, a mesh of linework can show depth and communicate movement and transitions.

INFORMATION DIAGRAMS

ORGANIZING LOGISTICS CAN IMPACT ARCHITECTURE'S FORM. The technical details that guide flows and operations can have immense bearing on how architecture is formed and developed. Diagramming a project's information has increasing agency—especially in public buildings, institutions and landscapes.

OMA's diagrams of the Seattle Public Library show how the architecture responds to the organization of the library collection

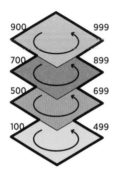

The first diagram explains the beginning

...and shows how architecture accommodates organization

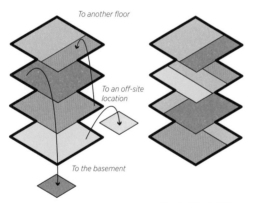

But as the collection expands, materials no longer fit the building

The building's flat, stacked floors disrupt the collection

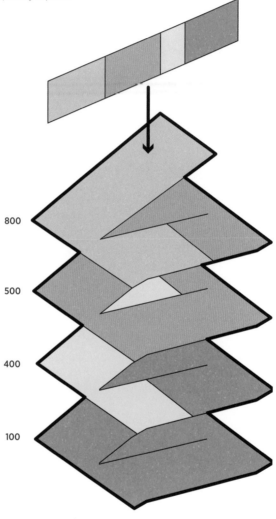

"Data structures can themselves be seen to operate as both the context of, and model for, the practices of the architect." —Brett Steele

ARCHITECTURE OF INFORMATION
Architecture engages identity through building design, but increasingly architecture engages communication through an institution's practices. How does the diagram absorb, organize and transform identity, culture and physical space?

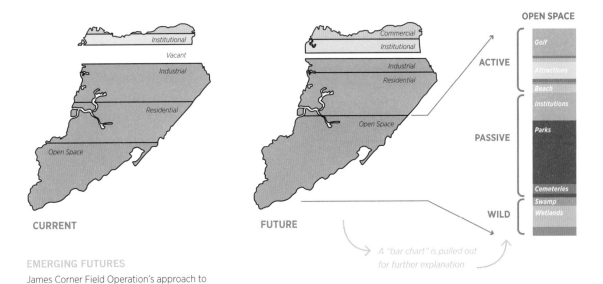

OPEN SPACE

ACTIVE
- Golf
- Attractions
- Beach

PASSIVE
- Institutions
- Parks
- Cemeteries

WILD
- Swamp
- Wetlands

CURRENT

FUTURE

*A "bar chart" is pulled out
for further explanation*

EMERGING FUTURES
James Corner Field Operation's approach to
Freshkills Park addressed how the site would
transform from landfill to community park.

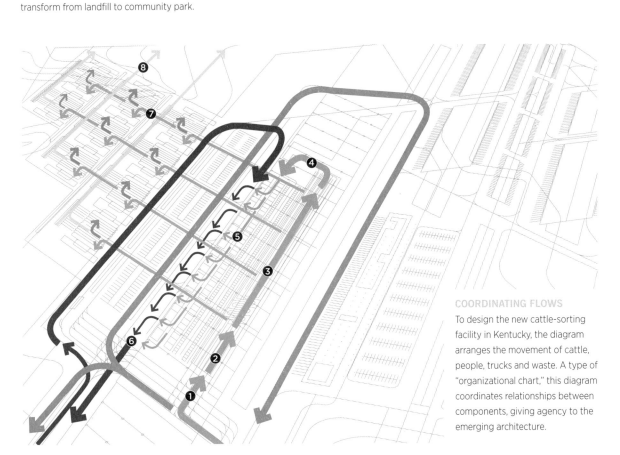

COORDINATING FLOWS
To design the new cattle-sorting
facility in Kentucky, the diagram
arranges the movement of cattle,
people, trucks and waste. A type of
"organizational chart," this diagram
coordinates relationships between
components, giving agency to the
emerging architecture.

*"Waste land" diagram proposes the movement
of cattle, people, trucks and manure*

THE PRODUCTION OF COLOR

DIFFERENT TOOLS INFLUENCE COLOR PRODUCTION. As technologies
have changed, so have the way colors are produced and viewed. Mixing paints or
selecting swatches on the computer impacts color's context.

TRADITIONAL / RYB

In the **traditional color wheel**,
primary colors yellow, blue and red
mix to form all colors. In this model,
white is the absence of all color.

*RYB, too, is
a subtractive
color model*

Secondary colors
are the product of
two **primary colors.**

Tertiary colors
result when mixing
sequential **primary
and secondary colors.**

**Complementary
colors** are opposite
one another on the
color wheel.

YELLOW
primary

YELLOW ORANGE
tertiary

YELLOW GREEN
tertiary

Split
complements

ORANGE
secondary

GREEN
secondary

○ Triadic colors

BLUE
GREEN
tertiary

RED
ORANGE
tertiary

Analogous

RED
primary

BLUE
primary

RED
PURPLE
tertiary

BLUE PURPLE
tertiary

PURPLE
secondary

■ **Split complements**
use the two colors
adjacent to the base
complement.

○ **Triadic colors** are
evenly spaced around
the color wheel.

● **Analogous colors**
are sequential on the
color wheel.

ART HISTORY
Reds, blues and yellows are present
in earlier diagrams, which relied on
the RYB model to mix paints.

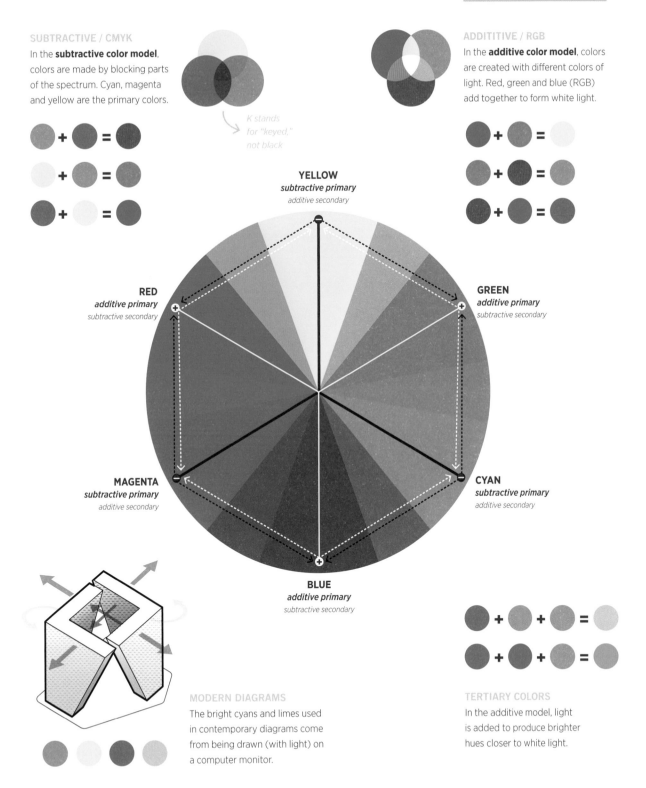

SUBTRACTIVE / CMYK

In the **subtractive color model**, colors are made by blocking parts of the spectrum. Cyan, magenta and yellow are the primary colors.

● + ● = ●

● + ● = ●

● + ● = ●

K stands for "keyed," not black

ADDITITIVE / RGB

In the **additive color model**, colors are created with different colors of light. Red, green and blue (RGB) add together to form white light.

● + ● = ●

● + ● = ●

● + ● = ●

YELLOW
subtractive primary
additive secondary

RED
additive primary
subtractive secondary

GREEN
additive primary
subtractive secondary

MAGENTA
subtractive primary
additive secondary

CYAN
subtractive primary
additive secondary

BLUE
additive primary
subtractive secondary

MODERN DIAGRAMS

The bright cyans and limes used in contemporary diagrams come from being drawn (with light) on a computer monitor.

TERTIARY COLORS

In the additive model, light is added to produce brighter hues closer to white light.

● + ● + ● = ●

● + ● + ● = ●

ALL OF THE ABOVE

JANETTE KIM, PRINCIPAL / DIRECTOR, COLUMBIA UNIVERSITY URBAN LANDSCAPE LAB / NEW YORK, NY

JANETTE KIM is an architectural designer, researcher and educator based in New York City. She is principal of All of the Above, a design practiced based in Brooklyn, and a faculty member at the Columbia University GSAPP, where she edits ARPA Journal, directs the Applied Research Practices in Architecture initiative and co-directs the Urban Landscape Lab. Janette's research work focuses on design and ecology in relationship to public representation, interest and debate. Janette holds a Masters of Architecture from Princeton University and a Bachelor of Arts from Columbia University.

GRAPHIC DESIGN FOR ARCHITECTS: How do you use diagrams to organize your design research?

JANETTE KIM: Much of my work is research-based, and uses graphics to draw out spaces, arguments and ideas in relationship to space.

GDA: What kinds of drawings do you use to describe your research?

JK: One example comes from a master plan we created for the Fall Kill, a creek in Poughkeepsie.

When we started, Poughkeepsie residents were largely unaware of the creek. It was boarded up and tucked behind private properties, and didn't have a physical presence in the city. We started the project by asking how the creek could play a greater role in Poughkeepsie's everyday life. I didn't know the city well yet, so I posed a naive question to our collaborators: "What are the neighborhoods in Poughkeepsie?" To my surprise, the response was that there weren't any.

If communities don't coalesce around neighborhoods, how do they organize politically? We mapped schools, child support infrastructures, social services, churches and retail environments. We looked for evidence of collective interest and sought to reveal links between people

RESIDENTS
PLAYGROUND + PARKING LOT TIMESHARE

EXISTING CONDITION:
narrow with with a wall

GREEN INFRASTRUCTURE:
permeable pavers

URBAN IMPACT:
dish-based improvements

SHARED
HOT TUB
+
BIRD BATH

2

3

and spaces that, when strengthened, could motivate Poughkeepsie residents to advocate for the creek and feel comfortable using new public spaces on its banks. We developed these observations through layered research documents that related information we were finding in GIS databases, city documents, direct site observations and from our own conversations with residents.

GDA: It sounds as if these layered drawings were actually maps.

JK: Yes, I see these research drawings more as maps than as diagrams. Since there are few spaces in Poughkeepsie that

we would traditionally associate with the public realm—parks, public squares, etc.— we had to identify less visible phenomena to understand the city. Here's a simple example: to get to and from the city's only public high school, kids walk or bike long distances across many other pathways— ones shared by workers getting to the train station, and residents who use bus lines to reach suburban supermarkets. These dense pathways were quite invisible; you would never know to look for them. But they provided the perfect sites for parks, markets and nurseries along the creek that could support after-school programs, or activate spaces that looked neglected but were actually in frequent use.

↑ **TOOL KITS**

1–3: A User's Guide to the Fall Kill Creek, *Urban Landscape Lab, PAUSE, Landmine Studio and eDesign Dynamics*

4–6: Pinterest Headquarters, *All of the Above / First Office*
    4: Organizational diagrams
    5: Models
    6: Ground-floor plan

7–8: Underdome, *Janette Kim and Erik Carver with the Urban Landscape Lab.*

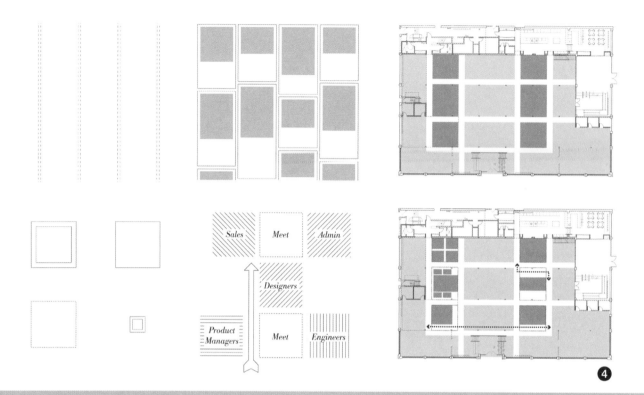

GDA: What's the difference between a map and a diagram?

JK: I've heard diagrams defined as a set of instructions. In this sense, the diagram is a drawing that lays the groundwork for future action, or defines an abstract process in geometric terms.

At the architectural scale, I use diagrams to test the organizational and programmatic logic of physical spaces. In our design for Pinterest's headquarters, we encountered a curious overlap between the visual structure of the Pinterest website, the Human Resources "diagram" of the company's organizational structure, and the plan of the office workplaces. Throughout our design process we constantly moved between these three discussions. To start, we made simple diagrams to prompt a conversation with the client about interactions among staff members. At Pinterest, designers, engineers and product managers work in close collaboration while maintaining their own disciplinary methods. We wanted to understand how people combine and separate to see how we could create opportunities for informal exchange and independent focus. Accordingly, we designed a kind of catalog of strange objects—a super huge table, a house-shaped volume sliced off at two sides, and so on—that would be built within an open floor plan and require people to invent new ways of organizing a meeting, occupying a war room, coming together for a collective lunch or throwing a party at the bar. The floor plans, in turn, used grid lines pointing in different directions to indicate where crossovers among disciplinary spaces could occur, and to locate acoustically sequestered spaces within the open office.

What's so brilliant about Pinterest's website is that they created a grid with a consistent width but a variable height, effectively allowing the combination of any kind of media. The site's engineering structure allows for cross-referencing through an infinite number of taxonomic frameworks. For example, you can pin an image of "pink football helmets," and the image could belong to the category "pink" and the category "football." We love that about the website, and we thought that's what the architecture should do. If you look at a floor plan cut three feet above ground, you'll see an array of desks that extends across the whole space. If you cut the plan at five feet you'll see team spaces emerge within visual and acoustic enclosures. At 12 feet you'll see the spaces all connected again, this time through lighting infrastructure, data cables and fire suppression. At all levels, you'd see a very consistent grid across the space that enables the formation of Pinterest teams in

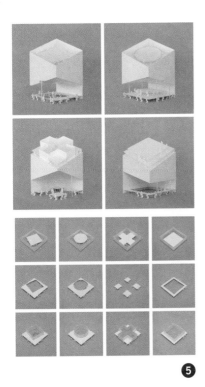

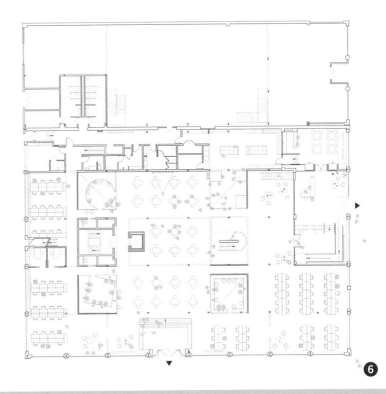

5

6

unexpected ways. So this was a case where the diagram was important to our work—the diagram was spatial but it also guided the company's organizational structure and working methods.

The Pinterest and Poughkeepsie drawings are quite different. In the former, we use the literal pattern of the organizational diagram to provoke unusual social organizations. In Poughkeepsie, we were drawing invisible actions. The geometry shown in our research drawings wasn't directly significant to the design, but did help us play with program and locate significant sites.

GDA: The diagram is an active design participant, it's a communication device between yourself and the design—it's a tool to help you as you're working. Versus a map is something you're uncovering as you draw your research.

JK: Once we established an idea for the Poughkeepsie master plan, we found that we needed a different visual language to provoke future action. Poughkeepsie's municipal government has demonstrated zero interest in supporting public space. So, despite our personal politics, we knew that a public space initiative would only happen if it were privately funded. It became clear to us that we needed to work with residents, small businesses, churches and schools along the creek, and we worked with our client, Clearwater, a non-profit environmental advocacy group, to lead the public to action.

GDA: A kind of "public action" diagram?

JK: We created signs at every major bridge across the creek that connected information about neighboring organizations to the waterway's ecology

and history. We also made a book that we called *The User's Guide to the Fall Kill Creek,* which offered ideas for property owners and tenants to activate spaces along the creek. If you're a church, for example, you could take advantage of these suggestions to use your parking lot for outdoor services or performances. It was fun for us to draw these options and to imagine different uses along the creek. The manual became a way for us to connect to different audiences, and Clearwater was able to get a grant from the EPA to host workshops with local residents.

GDA: Does the *Underdome* project leverage diagrams?

JK: I think *Underdome* builds upon a tradition of drawing that is interested less in a descriptive or operative diagram and more in the interpretation of a found

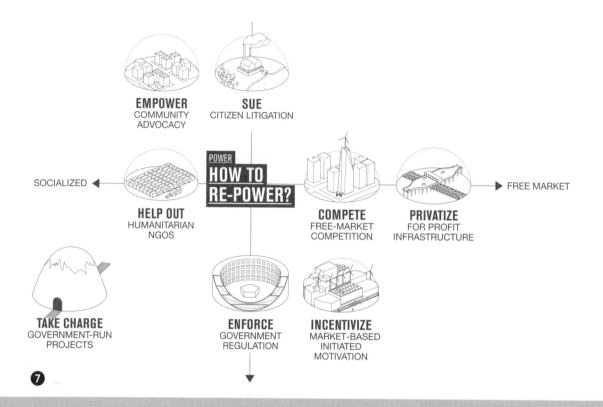

EMPOWER
COMMUNITY
ADVOCACY

SUE
CITIZEN LITIGATION

POWER
**HOW TO
RE-POWER?**

SOCIALIZED ◄

► FREE MARKET

HELP OUT
HUMANITARIAN
NGOS

COMPETE
FREE-MARKET
COMPETITION

PRIVATIZE
FOR PROFIT
INFRASTRUCTURE

TAKE CHARGE
GOVERNMENT-RUN
PROJECTS

ENFORCE
GOVERNMENT
REGULATION

INCENTIVIZE
MARKET-BASED
INITIATED
MOTIVATION

7

space. In *Learning from Las Vegas* or *Made in Tokyo,* for example, there is an attempt to use the map (in Robert Venturi, Denise Scott Brown and Steven Izenour's case) or the axonometric drawing (in Atelier Bow Wow's case) to develop a new theory about architectural design.

Similarly, *Underdome*—a website and forthcoming publication that compares contending attitudes towards energy reform—draws out existing buildings, sites and technologies in a very dry way. But we depart from the *Learning From* paradigm by framing conflicts among a set of examples. We framed the project as a debate so that readers can compare one ideological framework around energy against another. In the process we hope to open up new questions that challenge our assumptions about energy politics, and we hope to make explicit narratives of self-determination, lifestyle ideals and images of the city that lurk behind rhetoric.

To accomplish this, we draw the contradictions and oddities within any given energy scheme. For example, we are currently making a drawing of the Make It Right Foundation's efforts to build housing in the Lower Ninth Ward in New Orleans as an example of the humanitarian model of investment and recovery. We started by drawing the project as it is normally seen—as a close-up of the Morphosis building that floats. But we realized it would be much more interesting to show a different context, and zoomed out to show the houses in relationship to the levee, the flood gates and the hotels that people stayed in while they waited for new homes. This way we could show how humanitarian efforts are in fact reliant upon larger systems—infrastructures funded by the Army Corps of Engineers or FEMA, for example. We're trying to make the drawings a bit double-sided, so they could advocate for a position and critique it at the same time.

GDA: Perhaps the drawings of *Underdome* are better described as icons? The minute you zoom out and show more context they hold a different position. They become double-sided, they provoke a debate. Are the icons diagrams for conversation?

JK: Much of my work deals with architecture as a form of public engagement. Whether we are using maps in the Fall Kill master plan, organizational diagrams in the Pinterest headquarters or axonometrics in *Underdome*, drawings play a critical role in identifying and negotiating contending interests.

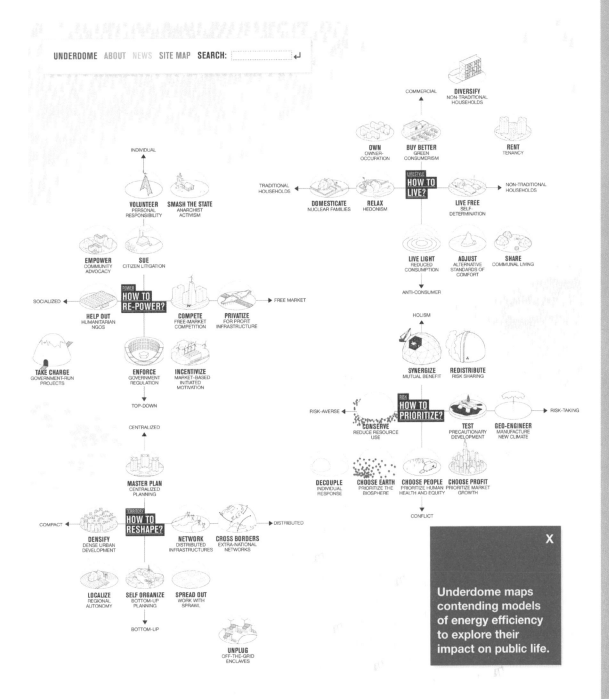

UNDERDOME ABOUT NEWS SITE MAP SEARCH: [   ] ↵

COMMERCIAL

DIVERSIFY
NON-TRADITIONAL
HOUSEHOLDS

OWN
OWNER-
OCCUPATION

BUY BETTER
GREEN
CONSUMERISM

RENT
TENANCY

INDIVIDUAL

TRADITIONAL
HOUSEHOLDS

LIFESTYLE
HOW TO
LIVE?

NON-TRADITIONAL
HOUSEHOLDS

VOLUNTEER
PERSONAL
RESPONSIBILITY

SMASH THE STATE
ANARCHIST
ACTIVISM

DOMESTICATE
NUCLEAR FAMILIES

RELAX
HEDONISM

LIVE FREE
SELF-
DETERMINATION

EMPOWER
COMMUNITY
ADVOCACY

SUE
CITIZEN LITIGATION

LIVE LIGHT
REDUCED
CONSUMPTION

ADJUST
ALTERNATIVE
STANDARDS OF
COMFORT

SHARE
COMMUNAL LIVING

SOCIALIZED

POWER
HOW TO
RE-POWER?

FREE MARKET

ANTI-CONSUMER

HELP OUT
HUMANITARIAN
NGOS

COMPETE
FREE-MARKET
COMPETITION

PRIVATIZE
FOR PROFIT
INFRASTRUCTURE

HOLISM

TAKE CHARGE
GOVERNMENT-RUN
PROJECTS

ENFORCE
GOVERNMENT
REGULATION

INCENTIVIZE
MARKET-BASED
INITIATED
MOTIVATION

SYNERGIZE
MUTUAL BENEFIT

REDISTRIBUTE
RISK SHARING

TOP-DOWN

RISK-AVERSE

RISK
HOW TO
PRIORITIZE?

RISK-TAKING

CENTRALIZED

CONSERVE
REDUCE RESOURCE
USE

TEST
PRECAUTIONARY
DEVELOPMENT

GEO-ENGINEER
MANUFACTURE
NEW CLIMATE

MASTER PLAN
CENTRALIZED
PLANNING

DECOUPLE
INDIVIDUAL
RESPONSE

CHOOSE EARTH
PRIORITIZE THE
BIOSPHERE

CHOOSE PEOPLE
PRIORITIZE HUMAN
HEALTH AND EQUITY

CHOOSE PROFIT
PRIORITIZE MARKET
GROWTH

COMPACT

TERRITORY
HOW TO
RESHAPE?

DISTRIBUTED

CONFLICT

DENSIFY
DENSE URBAN
DEVELOPMENT

NETWORK
DISTRIBUTED
INFRASTRUCTURES

CROSS BORDERS
EXTRA-NATIONAL
NETWORKS

X

LOCALIZE
REGIONAL
AUTONOMY

SELF ORGANIZE
BOTTOM-UP
PLANNING

SPREAD OUT
WORK WITH
SPRAWL

**Underdome maps
contending models
of energy efficiency
to explore their
impact on public life.**

BOTTOM-UP

UNPLUG
OFF-THE-GRID
ENCLAVES

❽

INFORMATION GRAPHICS

PIE CHARTS

PIE CHARTS ARE COMMON COMMUNICATION TOOLS. However, despite their ubiquity, they often misrepresent information. Paying attention to how information, text and color is presented in a piechart can have significant impact on their legibility.

Who is your favorite architecture theorist?

Black outlines separate the chart from the page and make it look heavy

Start at the top

Ⓧ OUT OF ORDER

It's intuitive to read a chart clockwise, top to bottom. However, the smallest segments are given the most prominence.

REORGANIZE PIECES

By putting the largest pie pieces at the top, the smallest segments are given the least prominence.

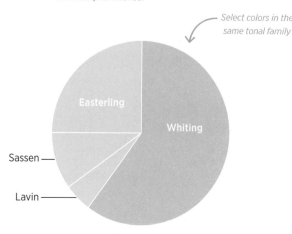

Select colors in the same tonal family

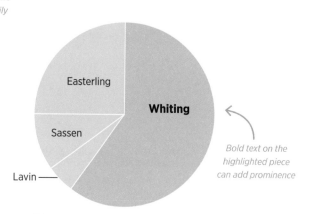

Bold text on the highlighted piece can add prominence

EFFECTIVE COLORS

Too many colors can be distracting. Allow one darker color to give prominence to the chart content you want to highlight.

✓ BLACK TEXT

Dark-colored text is always easier to read than white text on a darker background. Place labels in the center of each segment.

↓ EXPANDED INFORMATION

When expanding upon a pie chart, it is helpful to change representation forms. A segmented bar chart, rather than another pie chart, is more efficient at explaining proportions of a whole.

Who is your favorite architecture theorist?

Graduate students often cite writings by Sarah Whiting.

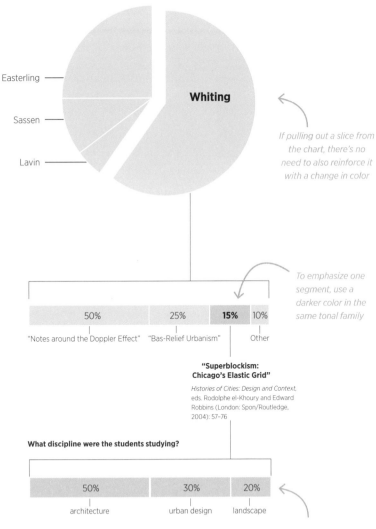

Easterling

Sassen

Lavin

Whiting

If pulling out a slice from the chart, there's no need to also reinforce it with a change in color

To emphasize one segment, use a darker color in the same tonal family

50%	25%	**15%**	10%

"Notes around the Doppler Effect"   "Bas-Relief Urbanism"   Other

"Superblockism: Chicago's Elastic Grid"

Histories of Cities: Design and Context, eds. Rodolphe el-Khoury and Edward Robbins (London: Spon/Routledge, 2004): 57–76

What discipline were the students studying?

50%	30%	20%

architecture   urban design   landscape

Unlike using multiple pie charts, expanding upon a segmented bar with another is clarifying

NOTES ON:

INFO-GRAPHIC RESOURCES

Dona M. Wong
Wall Street Journal Guide to Information Graphics
W.W. Norton & Co (2010)

Filled with great information and many helpful examples. The pie charts on these pages, as well as the information on number charts, have been synthesized from this publication.

Edward Tufte
Visual Explanations: Images and Quantities, Evidence and Narrative Graphics Press (1997)

All of Tufte's books are useful resources filled with historic examples of how information has been visualized and displayed.

Sandra Rendgen and Julius Weideman (eds.)
Information Graphics
Taschen (2012)

A tome of contemporary information graphics, filled with examples from the last decade.

PIE CHART VARIATIONS

PIE CHARTS DON'T HAVE TO BE ROUND. Their aim is to show percentages of a whole, not triangular wedges in circles. There are many ways proportions can be demonstrated visually.

Who is your favorite architect?
Denise Scott Brown is often recognized.

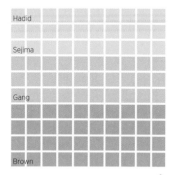

Each block equals one response, so it's easy to visualize individual answers within each percentage

→ SQUARES INSTEAD OF CIRCLES

Pie charts demonstrate proportions. In both of these square examples' responses are visualized through different-colored squares. Different-scaled answers are easier to see when there is a uniform geometry, or when units of measure are clearly delineated.

→ VARIATIONS ON A CIRCLE

Leaving the center open gives a lighter, more modern feel to a traditional pie-chart. It also allows percentages to be stacked against one another to work as a bar graph. An open center also leaves room for text.

Open space in the center provides an easy space for text

Similar to a bar graph

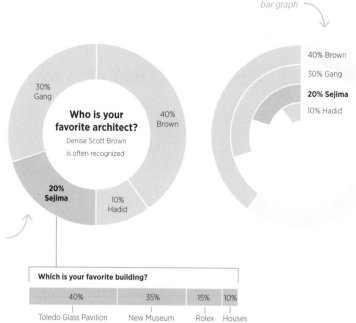

↓ PEAKS AND VALLEYS

Pie charts demonstrate proportions. In both of these square examples responses are visualized through different colored squares. Different scaled answers are easier to see when there is a uniform geometry, or when units of measure are clearly delineated.

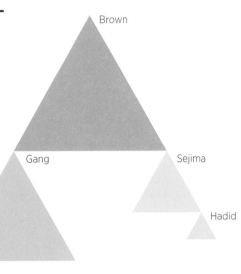

Architects' nationality is an example of **qualitative data**

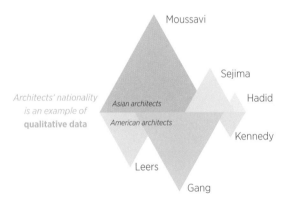

Sequencing by birthdate is an example of **quantatitve discrete data**

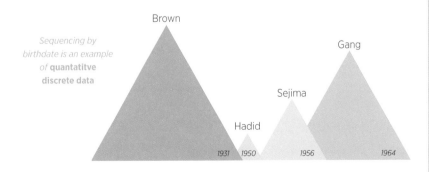

TYPES OF DATA

There are a few basic types of data to be aware of when representing information. Knowing what kind of information you have will make certain design decisions.

CATEGORY DATA

Information that isn't measured with a number—such as male or female—is known as **qualitative data**. This information could be demonstrated within a graph by using different types of colors or icons, for example.

NUMERICAL INFORMATION

Data that is a number is known as **quantitive data**. There are two types of this:

- **quantitive discrete**: Only certain numerical values are allowed, such as a round number. ***Number of buildings you've visited?* 103**

- **quantitive continuous**: Any number will work. ***How tall is that building?* 103.58 feet tall**

Knowing the difference between this information allows one to change data types to make better representations. For example, numbers in categories (0–10, 11–20, 21–30… etc) can look very different from continuous data (1, 2, 3…)

BAR CHARTS

PRESENTING DATA IS A DESIGN CHOICE. When given different datasets, think carefully about the best form to present information. Single bar charts might be the best way to illustrate a presentation. Layering information reveals a different story. Only show information that is relevant to the case you're trying to present.

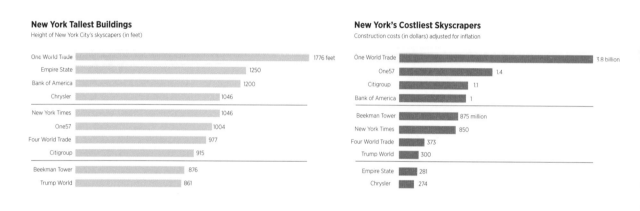

New York Tallest Buildings
Height of New York City's skyscapers (in feet)

One World Trade — 1776 feet
Empire State — 1250
Bank of America — 1200
Chrysler — 1046
New York Times — 1046
One57 — 1004
Four World Trade — 977
Citigroup — 915
Beekman Tower — 876
Trump World — 861

New York's Costliest Skyscrapers
Construction costs (in dollars) adjusted for inflation

One World Trade — 3.8 billion
One57 — 1.4
Citigroup — 1.1
Bank of America — 1
Beekman Tower — 875 million
New York Times — 850
Four World Trade — 373
Trump World — 300
Empire State — 281
Chrysler — 274

Cost of New York's Tallest Skyscrapers

Construction costs (in dollars) compared to building height

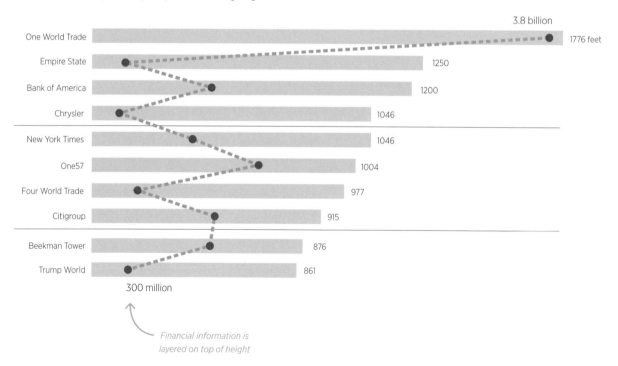

One World Trade — 3.8 billion — 1776 feet
Empire State — 1250
Bank of America — 1200
Chrysler — 1046
New York Times — 1046
One57 — 1004
Four World Trade — 977
Citigroup — 915
Beekman Tower — 876
Trump World — 861

300 million

Financial information is layered on top of height

NEW YORK'S TALLEST AND COSTLIEST BUILDINGS

Height and Construction Costs

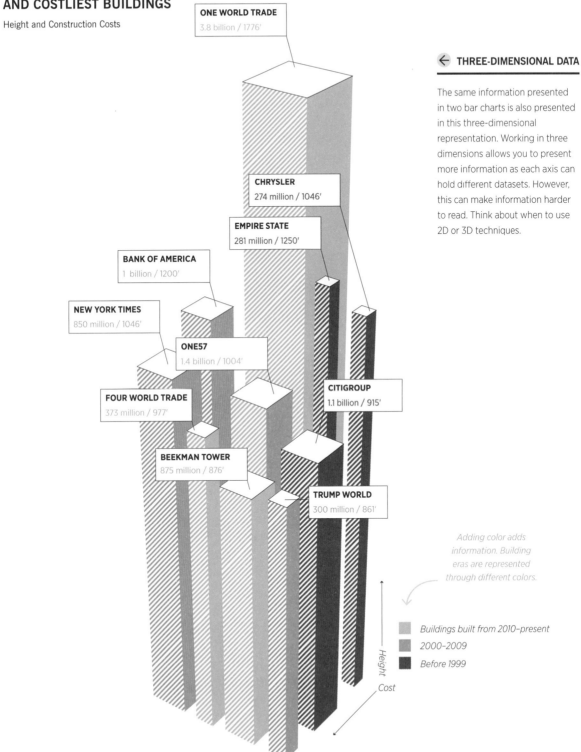

ONE WORLD TRADE
3.8 billion / 1776'

CHRYSLER
274 million / 1046'

EMPIRE STATE
281 million / 1250'

BANK OF AMERICA
1 billion / 1200'

NEW YORK TIMES
850 million / 1046'

ONE57
1.4 billion / 1004'

FOUR WORLD TRADE
373 million / 977'

CITIGROUP
1.1 billion / 915'

BEEKMAN TOWER
875 million / 876'

TRUMP WORLD
300 million / 861'

← **THREE-DIMENSIONAL DATA**

The same information presented in two bar charts is also presented in this three-dimensional representation. Working in three dimensions allows you to present more information as each axis can hold different datasets. However, this can make information harder to read. Think about when to use 2D or 3D techniques.

Adding color adds information. Building eras are represented through different colors.

Height

Cost

Buildings built from 2010–present

2000–2009

Before 1999

PIE CHARTS VERSUS BAR CHARTS

NOT ALL CHARTS PRESENT INFORMATION IN THE SAME WAY. Knowing which chart
to use to present information is as important as knowing how to present information clearly.
The way information is shaped and the form it takes is a significant part of its communication.

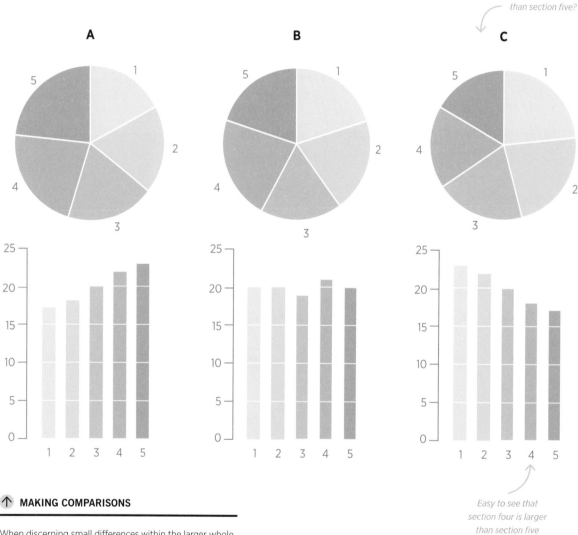

Is section four larger than section five?

A   B   C

Easy to see that section four is larger than section five

↑ **MAKING COMPARISONS**

When discerning small differences within the larger whole,
bar charts are far more effective than pie charts. When
information is presented in bar charts, one can easily make
comparisons between the data. If presented in a pie chart,
each wedge can appear to be the same size.

↓ SIDE BY SIDE

When trying to understand difference, making direct, side-by-side comparisons helps indicate change. Trying to understand the differences between bar lengths when they are separated is much harder than when they are placed directly next to each other.

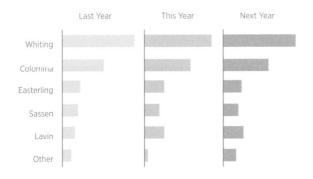

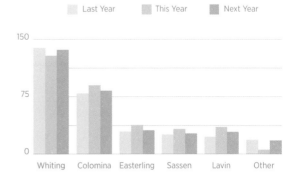

✕ NO COMPARISON
It is difficult to see the difference between the bars for last year, this year and next year.

✓ EASY TO COMPARE
When condensed next to each other, it is easy to see the differences between each bar graph.

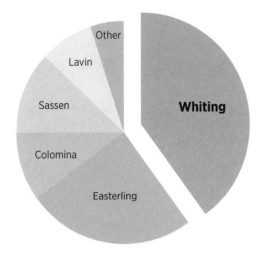

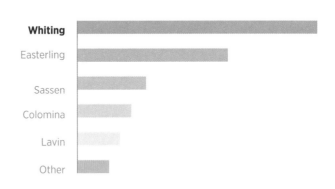

 SMALLER SEGMENTS
Its easy to see the largest piece of the pie chart, but hard to understand the differences between smaller segments.

 EASY TO COMPARE
Our eyes are able to understand the difference between pieces when there is a clear datum.

PRESENTING NUMBERS

DESPITE BEING STRAIGHTFORWARD, NUMBERS ARE HARD TO PRESENT. Numbers, like words, can quickly become a wash of indecipherable data. Shaping numbers with line breaks, shading, type weights and alignment can help shape the presentation of numerical

Heavier lead line makes an effective division between headers and data

Name	Data	Data	Data	Data
Project 1	0.0	0.0	0.0	0.0
Project 2	0.0	0.0	0.0	0.0
Project 3	0.0	0.0	0.0	0.0
Project 4	0.0	0.0	0.0	0.0
Project 5	0.0	0.0	0.0	0.0
Project 6	0.0	0.0	0.0	0.0
Project 7	0.0	0.0	0.0	0.0
Project 8	0.0	0.0	0.0	0.0

Name	Data	Data	Data	Data
Project 1	0.0	0.0	0.0	0.0
Project 2	0.0	0.0	0.0	0.0
Project 3	0.0	0.0	0.0	0.0
Project 4	0.0	0.0	0.0	0.0
Project 5	0.0	0.0	0.0	0.0
Project 6	0.0	0.0	0.0	0.0
Project 7	0.0	0.0	0.0	0.0
Project 8	0.0	0.0	0.0	0.0

✕ DISTRACTING LINES

Too many lines cause heavy divisions between cells, making information hard to read.

✕ MOIRE EFFECT

In small charts, alternating zones of dark and light lines appear busy. Readers can easily scan information without these colored divisions.

Column label is centered over the number

Name	Data	Data	Data	Data
Project 1	0.0	15.0	0.0	0.0
Project 2	0.0	14.0	0.0	0.0
Project 3	0.0	13.0	0.0	0.0
Project 4	0.0	12.0	0.0	0.0
Project 5	0.0	11.0	0.0	0.0
Project 6	0.0	10.0	0.0	0.0
Project 7	0.0	9.0	0.0	0.0
Project 8	0.0	8.0	0.0	0.0
Project 9	0.0	7.0	0.0	0.0
Project 10	0.0	6.0	0.0	0.0
Project 11	0.0	5.0	0.0	0.0
Project 12	0.0	4.0	0.0	0.0

Name	Data	Data		Data
Project 1	0.0		15.0	0.0
Project 2	0.0		14.0	0.0
Project 3	0.0		13.0	0.0
Project 4	0.0		12.0	0.0
Project 5	0.0		11.0	0.0
Project 6	0.0		10.0	0.0
Project 7	0.0		9.0	0.0
Project 8	0.0		8.0	0.0
Project 9	0.0		7.0	0.0
Project 10	0.0		6.0	0.0
Project 11	0.0		5.0	0.0
Project 12	0.0		4.0	0.0

✓ SMALL GUIDES

Thin lines every three to five lines can help readers scan across the table. Shading can be used to highlight important data.

✓ CHART IN A TABLE

Charts are more memorable than numbers, so when possible use a chart to represent the important information.

EFFECTIVE COMPARISONS

When presenting multiple data sets in one chart, it's easier to compare information vertically than to make comparisons horizontally.

Cluttered text is especially hard to read white on black

CHART TITLE
OVERVIEW OF THE INFORMATION PRESENTED IN THE CHART

Never set text at an angle

	Project 1	Project 2	Project 3
Budget	10,000	20,000	30,000
Cost / sq. foot	60	80	100
Time	100	200	300

 CLUTTERED INFORMATION

Text is presented in distracting ways— bold, italics, reversed, even at an angle. The chart's purpose (to compare data between companies) is hard to understand.

A simple headline explains the graph without overwhelming

Chart Title
Overview of the information presented in the chart

	Budget	Cost / sq. ft	Time
Project 1	10,000	60	100
Project 2	20,000	80	200
Project 3	30,000	100	300

 EASIER TO READ

The chart is organized around information pertaining to each project, rather than information about budgets, costs and time.

It's OK to center small numbers

 Whole numbers are left-justified

Name	Data
Project 1	5000
Project 2	700
Project 3	50
Project 4	3

Align whole numbers to the right

Name	Data
Project 1	5000
Project 2	700
Project 3	50
Project 4	3

 Decimal points are left-justified

Name	Data
Project 1	12.31
Project 2	1.22
Project 3	89.8
Project 4	7.0

Decimals aligned above the other

Name	Data
Project 1	12.3
Project 2	1.2
Project 3	89.8
Project 4	7.0

 ALIGNING WHOLE NUMBERS

If designing whole numbers (figures without decimal points), justify them to the right as it is easier to read the different between larger and smaller numbers.

 **ALIGNING DECIMALS**

Decimal numbers should never be aligned flush left or right, but rather should have their decimal points line up.

FLOW CHARTS

GRAPHICS GIVE SHAPE TO ENTIRE SETS OF INFORMATION. However, within each dataset, hierarchies of information are embedded. How are these more complex relationships revealed? How does a drawing demonstrate information's entirety as well as its details?

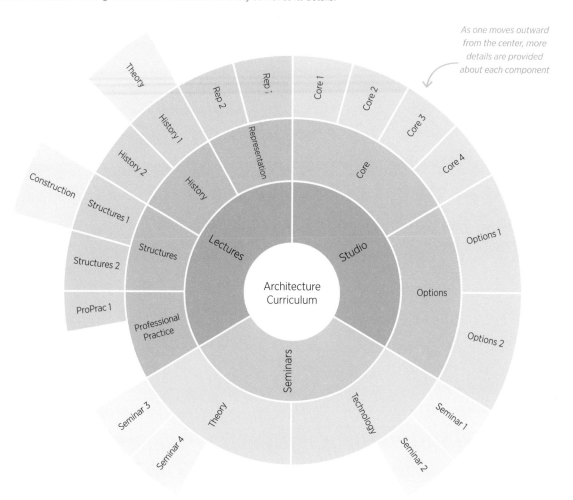

As one moves outward from the center, more details are provided about each component

↑ **EXPANDING OUTWARDS**

Some charts indicate different types of relationships between data segments. In the center of this chart is a title, then a set of information that breaks the previous segment into smaller pieces. Each ring of the chart shows a subset of the previous information.

Areas of Graduate Study

Number of Students Earning Design Degrees

← **BREAKING GROUPS APART**

Similar to the graph on the opposite page, this flow chart shows how a set of information can be broken into different parts. How can information be designed to show its subsets, as well as its entirety?

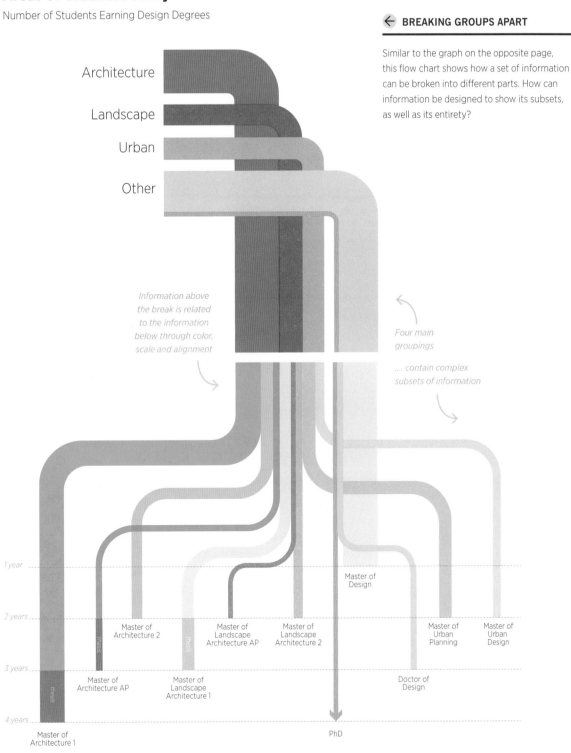

Architecture

Landscape

Urban

Other

Information above the break is related to the information below through color, scale and alignment

Four main groupings

.... contain complex subsets of information

1 year

Master of Design

2 years

Master of Architecture 2

Master of Landscape Architecture AP

Master of Landscape Architecture 2

Master of Urban Planning

Master of Urban Design

3 years

Master of Architecture AP

Master of Landscape Architecture 1

Doctor of Design

4 years

Master of Architecture 1

PhD

thesis

FILSON AND ROHRBACHER

ANNE FILSON, PRINCIPAL / LEXINGTON, KY

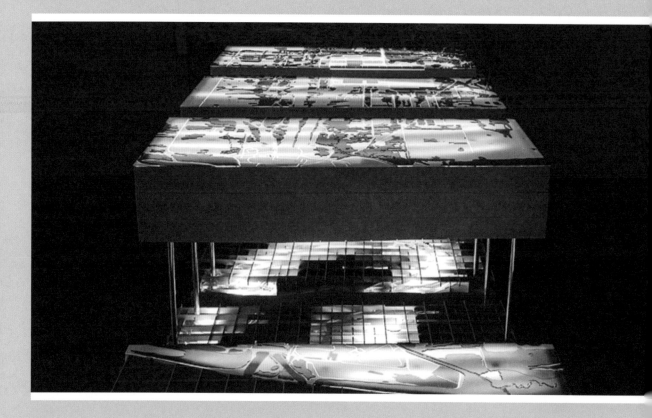

ANNE FILSON *is a principal of Filson and Rohrbacher, an architecture, design and research firm. She is an architect, researcher and educator, who has pursued the critical practice of architecture through a wide range of projects for many types of clients. She was a Project Architect at OMA / Rem Koolhaas, pursued Strategic / Design Consulting for IDEO's Smart Space Practice, and worked at both large corporate and small design-centric firms. She currently teaches design and professional practice at the University of Kentucky, and holds a MArch degree from Columbia University and a BA in Art History from Smith College.*

GRAPHIC DESIGN FOR ARCHITECTS: You've been part of a few on-going research projects focused on issues relevant to micropolitan communities. What are the challenges in designing these types of environments?

ANNE FILSON: Micropolitan is a relatively new designation that describes towns between 25,000 and 55,000 people. They're too big to be considered small towns, and they have more economic diversity than small towns do. Most micropolitan communities on the East and West coast are absorbed into other larger metro regions, but the Midwest has an abundance of micropolitan centers. Many of these centers have lost population with their industrial base.

In the case of the Henderson Studio, which was part of the Kentucky River Studios Program at the University of Kentucky, Matthijs Bouw of One Architecture and I approached the project from a planning standpoint. We looked at Henderson's physical infrastructure, buildings, landscape, river, etc and mapped all of these physical elements. But we also drew on other kinds of intangible information.

We looked at flows of materials and commodities moving in and out of Henderson: coal, aluminum, energy, other capital that was moving through the town. In analyzing the geographical disposition of these economic exchanges, we sought to understand and to question what could drive a new era of prosperity. We

complemented this with anthropological research, and interviewed a diverse cross-section of the community to understand better Henderson's culture.

GDA: Do you need different ways of representing these un-dense cities?

AF: Dense urban centers, such as Manhattan, Rome or Chicago, are easily understood by figure–ground. But when drawing—and designing for—a city that is not dense, that has much less "figure" to "ground," you have to develop other mapping techniques. You have to find other things to draw, find other ways of measuring and drawing scale so these un-dense cities still read as "settled."

Just drawing the strip mall, the parking lot and the farm road won't tell you enough about the community you're investigating. You have to start looking at larger distances and disparate concentrations in order to understand the micropolitan environment. There is density in these locations, physical settlement seems spread further apart but non–physical flows of social exchange, materials and energy become elements are more prominent. When you recognize this form of dispersal, you also realize the different ways these places are connected. The drawing project then is to describe the intensity of flows between concentrations, not the object of the city's figure–ground. Instead you are drawing and designing the forces around the centers.

↑ **TESTING GROUND**

The series of models combined scaled architectural representations with information from geologists. Developed with innovative printing methods, these models are interactive tools for community stakeholders. Participants can draw and diagram directly on the models, changing pieces to test different ideas. The models serve as a way to host conversations, rather than document building form.

Photos by Magnus Lindqvist, Glint Studio

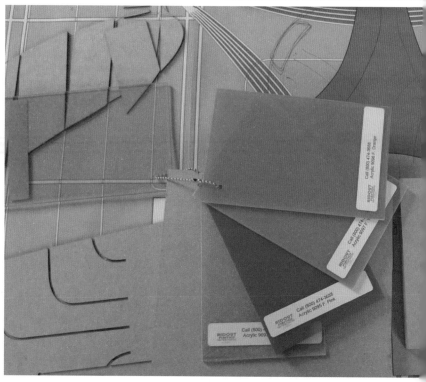

GDA: Was this challenging to describe to the students?

AF: Absolutely. Because the city was so unusual, and figure-ground plans weren't going to tell the interesting story, the students had to invent graphic conventions for their maps. They had to redraw their maps several times to try to find a way of describing the city. For example, we had a student draw an energy diagram that described the incredible intensity of power generated by the city. These maps recognized the intensity of Henderson—it just wasn't a human intensity, but rather one made from megawatts. After drawing that energy map, you start to see that this small city has a significant role in the state.

GDA: How were you able to help Paducah see itself differently?

AF: The Department of Energy, local government and other experts have all known about the sub-surface ground concentrations beneath the PGDP (Paducah Gaseous Diffusion Plant) in Paducah, KY. These concentrations were byproducts from decades of uranium enrichment during the Cold War. There has been no consensus on the problem or the remedy. Paducah's stakeholders have different understandings of the situation: geologists saw the condition as a spreadsheet of numbers; the Department of Energy viewed it as a public relations problem; the public believed it was something frightening; local government wondered if it would detract from future growth. Every group had a different point of view.

Similar to how we began in Henderson, Gary Rohrbacher started the project in

his studio by visualizing the physical information. No one had ever physically modeled or visualized the collected data before, so his funded research studio began by plotting the geologists' data points into a three-dimensional meshwork and sited it within the physical context of PGDP. This way one could see the collected information in relationship to existing topography, buildings, roads, the water table, etc.

With funding from the Department of Energy, Gary and I led a post-graduate research team to follow up the studio by building a digitally fabricated physical model of the PGDP site and the underground enrichment byproducts. We presented the model to the stakeholders. It was the first time any one of them had seen the data in a way they could understand. Visualizing this information brought the stakeholders onto the same

page because they started to understand the same things. We understood that after visualizing this data the city, scientists, engineers and developers could start building a consensus about the scope of the problem, and then about how to address it. We were pleased that the model and the drawings our research team developed facilitated these conversations.

Not everyone can read a spreadsheet, but everyone can read a physical model.

GDA: As the conversation evolved, how did the design of the models change?

AF: We led our research team to make several iterations of models. That first one modeled the site's physical components and documented what existed: the ground concentrations, buildings, river, water table, roads. This proved to be such a powerful

tool that the Department of Energy funded the development and production of further models. The first model documented the conditions—it had interchangeable parts, but it didn't move at the speed of the conversation. For the second model we decided to make a more interactive tool, something that could change at the speed of the conversation.

This next model facilitated the stakeholders' conversation about the ground concentration, monitoring and remediation, and scenarios for Paducah's development. We built the model out of plexiglass that could be written on and tagged—the buildings and roads were glued down, but everything else could move or be drawn on, crossed out, changed. We designed a tool kit to accompany the interactive model that included indelible china markers,

different identity markers, tags, scales and other plexiglass cut pieces to mark the conversation. This model helped facilitate conversations, to give the stakeholders a physical tool to envision alternative futures. In contrast to the first model that was about understanding what's there, this one gave community stakeholders agency in imagining and describing what could happen to the site.

Our research team built a third generation model that showed the PGDP site at a much larger scale. This scale made it possible to add more detailed information and a greater degree of mutability. We embedded small plexi rods that marked where the geologists made their boring holes to take measurements, from the original spreadsheet. We designed the model to be easily transported from site to site, updatable with new data and

intuitively usable by community groups, politicians, scientists and contractors.

We discovered an innovative printer by LexMark (a global printing company, based in Lexington, KY) to back-print multiple plexiglass layers with physical information, data, details and a grid to give a better sense of scale and measure. We designed the model to easily add or remove the plexiglass layers of information. So, as new data becomes available, the client can easily plot new layers and update the model with new information.

GDA: This gets back to the issue of apparent physicality. Much of the site's "figure" was determined by the chemical concentration under the ground surface. While these concentrations were very

present, they weren't visible. This physical condition would never show up if the studio only visualized figure–ground.

AF: Exactly. And that subterranean ground-figure was changing. As remediation changed the extent of the sub-surface contaminants, the scientists, engineers, contractors and government planners could use the model to communicate its retreat. They could note that the line of the plume would move, and as it changed it would open up new areas of the site for design and development.

GDA: The models you designed were visualizing different potentials rather than demonstrating specific solutions. Does this work reflect a different role for architects?

AF: What's fascinating is that this whole process took architects. The Department of Energy has invested billions to monitor and document the ground conditions, and never once were they able to adequately communicate the concentrations to PGDP's many stakeholders. We felt it was essential to use models to describe data and engage user participation—which is a different role for the architect. Some of this comes from my experience at OMA, where models are used internally to imagine alternatives, to test ideas quickly. We rejected the idea that the model was a presentation document to demonstrate the final design, and wanted the models to hold the conversation, to build consensus about what the design was. We used models to communicate to Rem, to each other, they were powerful

internal tools; but they also became tools to communicate to the client and other stakeholders. Gary and I approached PGDP the same way by making models about process, about understanding conditions, about imagining new futures. We took the PGDP models a step further than OMA, in that the model remains in flux, long after
it leaves the hands of the architect.

GDA: You asked the models to have an active role in the design process. How is this different from ways models are typically used?

AF: Models at the beginning can be a way to have a conversation—a step in the process versus a documentation of all of our decisions to hand down to the client.

Models can be a tool to communicate what is emerging.

OMA made models that are very graphic—representative of different ideas, programs, materials, porosities—which are different from models that serve as documents of the finished design. It goes back to the figure–ground discussion again. Those tools are useful to visualize form and the surrounding space. But these graphic models are about diagramming all of the other information that influences the proposed design.

I think the model serves as a way to visualize and describe all of the fluid, interactive decisions that go into a design project. For example at IIT, we had a 12-foot long model of the whole building and it was a very powerful document. We would use the model to talk to the

contractor about how the roof plane came together, or to explain the logic of material application to the local architect, or to show the client the logic of where the offices were located in relationship to circulation. The model visualizes relationships and design logics.

People who are engaged in big projects need ways to understand the complexities and the outcomes of these choices. At both OMA and for PGDP, we used architecture drawings and processes—diagrams, drawings, models—as the interface for complex issues that are moving, changing and are not static. For PGDP, Gary and I took further steps to design tools to enable stakeholders. Through the models they were not only able to understand the issues, they were able to find and have agency over them.

COORDINATING INFORMATION

MAPPING IS ABOUT GRAPHICALLY REPRESENTING INFORMATION. Choices about colors, line weights, textures, photographs and orientation are issues of how to catalyze information and give it agency, not just how to make it look good. How we are able to absorb information affects our choices, perceptions and connection to the world.

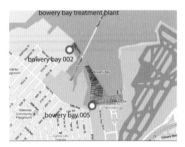

EXISTING MAPS

These are helpful working tools to hold and organize information but shouldn't be used as final graphics.

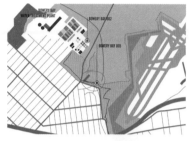

ADJUST TO GREY

The background map is simplified to grey linework while the proposed design is added in color.

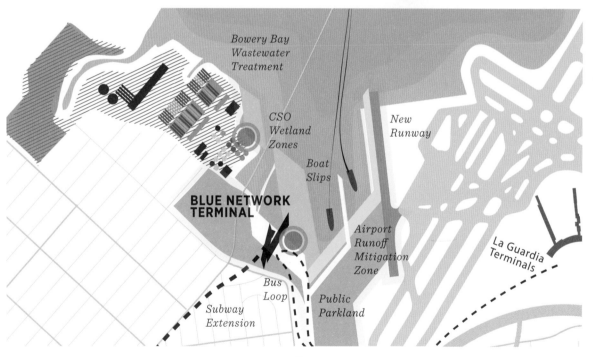

A light, transparent blue line washes the design perimeter, integrating the strong colors of the proposal into the map line weight

COLOR HIERARCHY

The map base is toned down even further while the main design subject is highlighted with stronger, more saturated colors. Typography and line weights also contribute to how the image is read and understood.

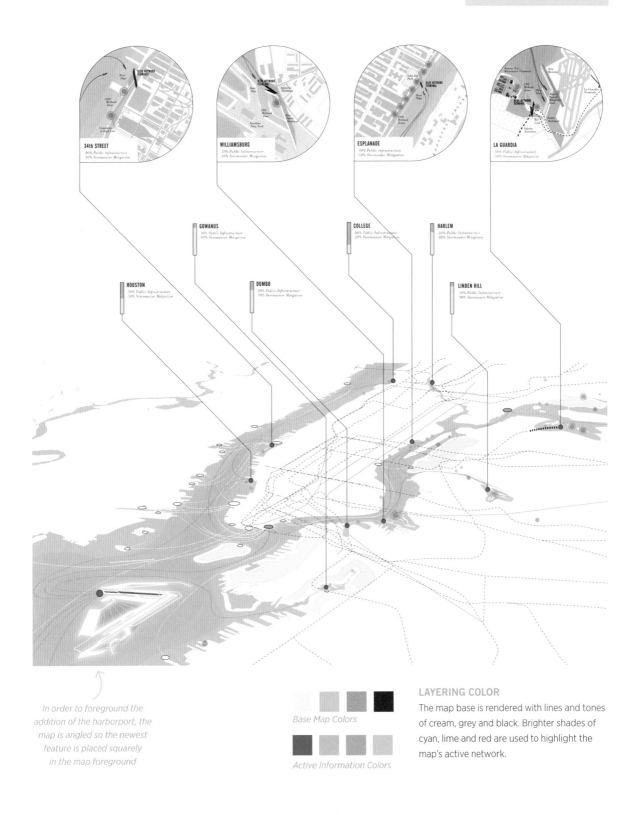

34th STREET
90% Public Infrastructure
10% Stormwater Mitigation

WILLIAMSBURG
30% Public Infrastructure
70% Stormwater Mitigation

ESPLANADE
40% Public Infrastructure
60% Stormwater Mitigation

LA GUARDIA
50% Public Infrastructure
50% Stormwater Mitigation

GOWANUS
10% Public Infrastructure
90% Stormwater Mitigation

COLLEGE
80% Public Infrastructure
20% Stormwater Mitigation

HARLEM
20% Public Infrastructure
80% Stormwater Mitigation

HOUSTON
50% Public Infrastructure
50% Stormwater Mitigation

DUMBO
30% Public Infrastructure
70% Stormwater Mitigation

LINDEN HILL
10% Public Infrastructure
90% Stormwater Mitigation

*In order to foreground the
addition of the harborport, the
map is angled so the newest
feature is placed squarely
in the map foreground*

Base Map Colors

Active Information Colors

LAYERING COLOR
The map base is rendered with lines and tones
of cream, grey and black. Brighter shades of
cyan, lime and red are used to highlight the
map's active network.

LAYERING INFORMATION

MAPS OVERLAY INFORMATION TO MAKE COMPARISONS BETWEEN ELEMENTS.
How you choose to organize the layers of information has an impact on how maps are read and understood. Graphics inform how information is prioritized.

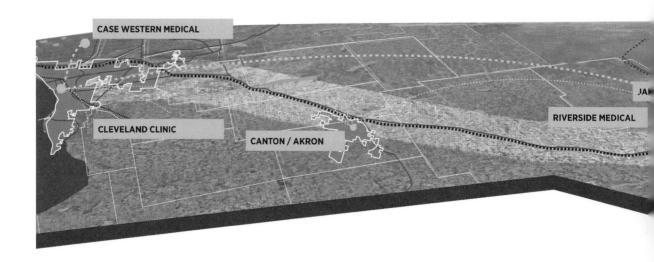

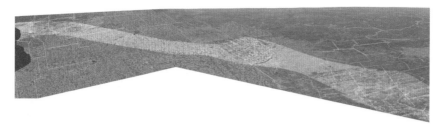

1 BASE INFORMATION
Some images just look better in black and white. The orange wood tones of the thin ply against the cool grey concrete are neutralized when the image is changed to black and white.

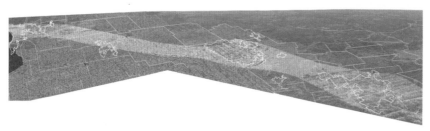

2 LINES GIVE SCALE
County and metro areas are added as white linework, giving the map scale and context.

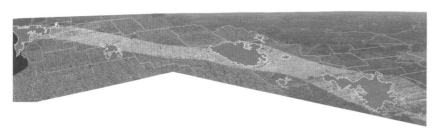

3 ADDING COLOR
Metro areas are filled in with a solid color. The satellite photo becomes more like a map when layers of drawing elements, such as lines, color and pattern are added.

↓ FINAL LAYER OF INFORMATION

Hospital locations and labels are added to the map.
Further line weight demonstrates the network that
exists between these sites.

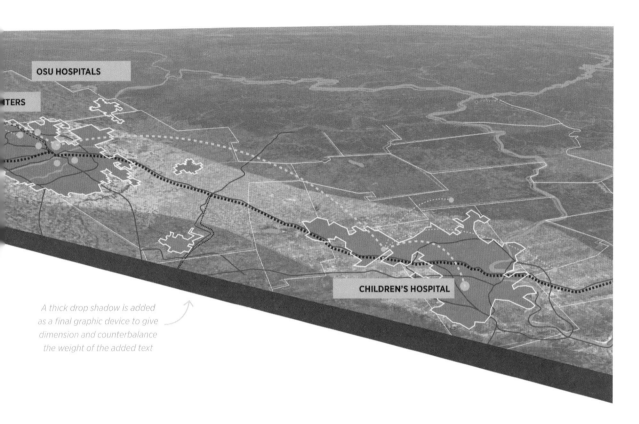

OSU HOSPITALS

TERS

CHILDREN'S HOSPITAL

*A thick drop shadow is added
as a final graphic device to give
dimension and counterbalance
the weight of the added text*

4 RIVERS AND ROADS
Highways and rivers are added
bringing additional scale and
atmosphere. These elements
provide color and detail which
enhance the map's intricacy.

5 RAILROAD
The proposed railroad is added
as a final layer. The line weight is
darker and heavier than other lines,
so its prominence is adjusted by
making it dashed (an appropriate
line treatment for a railroad).

LEVELS OF SPECIFICITY

MAPS CAN ONLY COMMUNICATE THEIR DATASET. Without good data, one cannot produce a good map. As datasets become more complex, graphic techniques must be enhanced to communicate the range and breadth of information.

IDENTIFY THE
CORN BELT

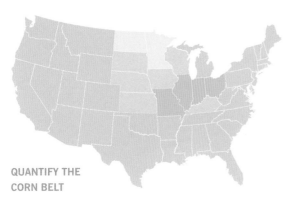

QUANTIFY THE
CORN BELT

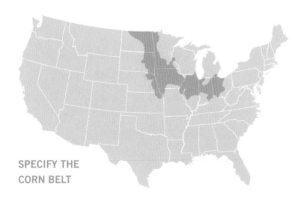

SPECIFY THE
CORN BELT

✔ **DETAILED DATASETS**
Mapping information about corn production at the county, rather than only at the state, scale brings specificity to a corn production map. At this level of detail, relationships to climate and environment can be made.

↓ BREADTH AND DETAIL

The Corn Belt is communicated in several ways. Its general location is given by the states outlined in darker grey. Details about each county's corn production is depicted through a range of colors. Pale yellow indicates smaller quanitites than deeper orange.

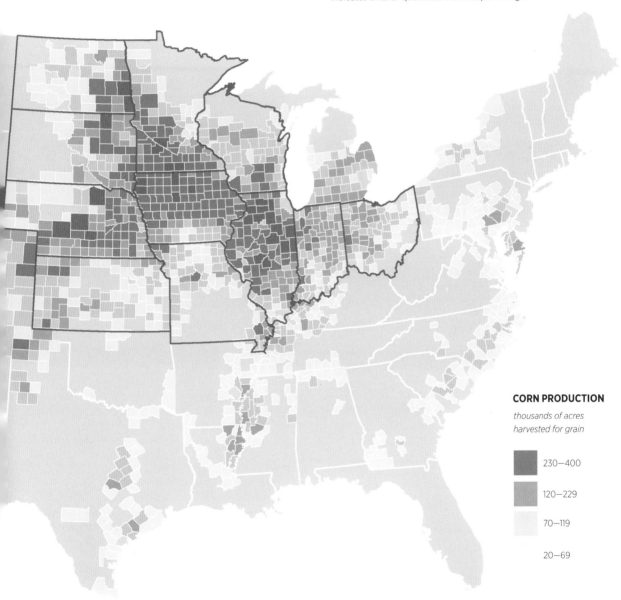

CORN PRODUCTION

thousands of acres harvested for grain

230—400
120—229
70—119
20—69

ENHANCING RELATIONSHIPS

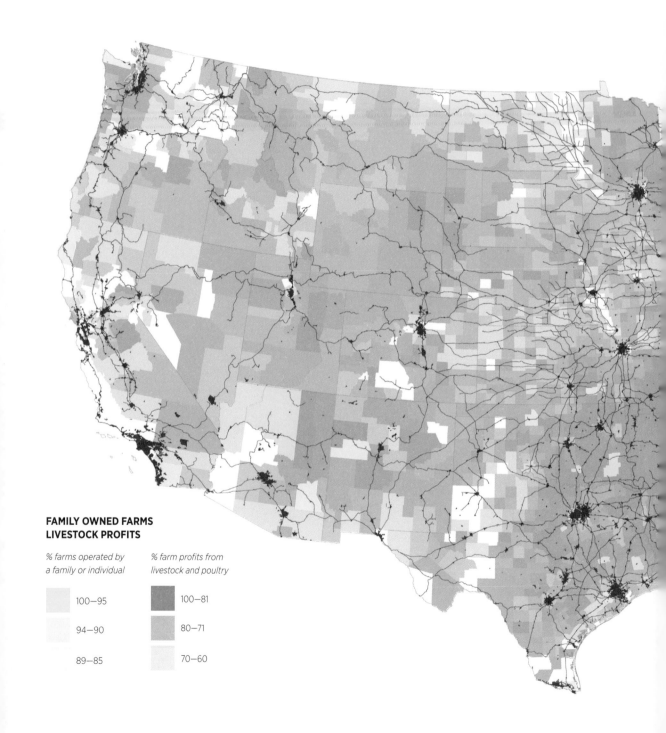

**FAMILY OWNED FARMS
LIVESTOCK PROFITS**

*% farms operated by
a family or individual*

*% farm profits from
livestock and poultry*

100—95

94—90

89—85

100—81

80—71

70—60

TRANSPARENCY
makes colors, and information, washed out and difficult to read

✓ **OVERPRINTING**
produces vibrant, interesting information that's clear to read

Wherever colors overlap, there is an overlapping of information

↓

NOTES ON:

BRIGHT COLORS

How do you set colors to overlap on top of one another and still look vibrant? Here's how.

FORGET ABOUT THE TRANSPARENCY TOOL

The first impulse to make colors read on top of one another is to change the transparency. This just makes work look lighter and unsaturated.

100% = solid   *50% = transparency*

OVERPRINT INSTEAD

Simulating the effects of overprinting helps work stay vibrant and rich.

50% pastels   *overprint*

The green made by changing each color's transparency is washed out and barely legible. The rich green produced by overprinting is vibrant and saturated. One can read clearly the combination of the two primary colors (aka: two primary sets of information).

AGGREGATING MARKS

AS IN ARCHITECTURAL DRAWINGS, LINES COMMUNICATE INTENTION.

Crafting a map's line weight allows for pieces of information to come forward or recede, for different areas to have focus, or for different parts of a map's information structure to communicate differently than others.

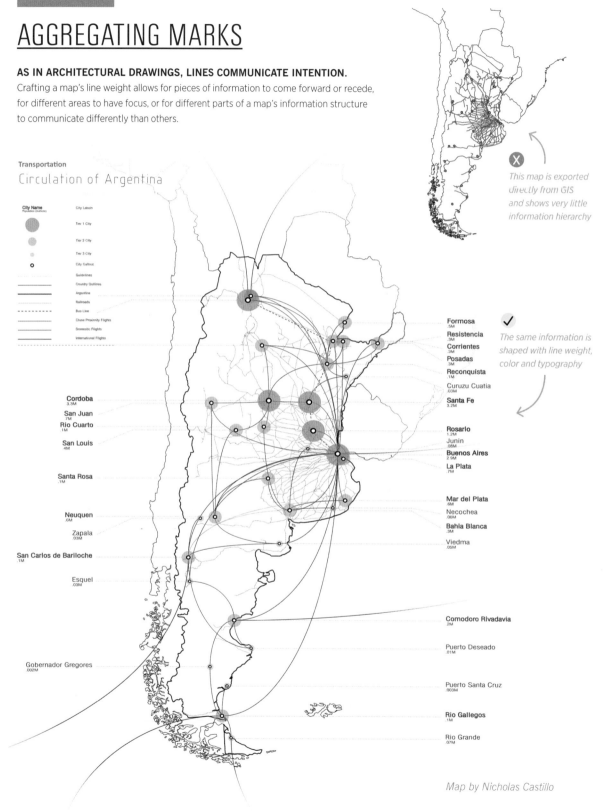

This map is exported directly from GIS and shows very little information hierarchy

The same information is shaped with line weight, color and typography

Transportation

Circulation of Argentina

Map by Nicholas Castillo

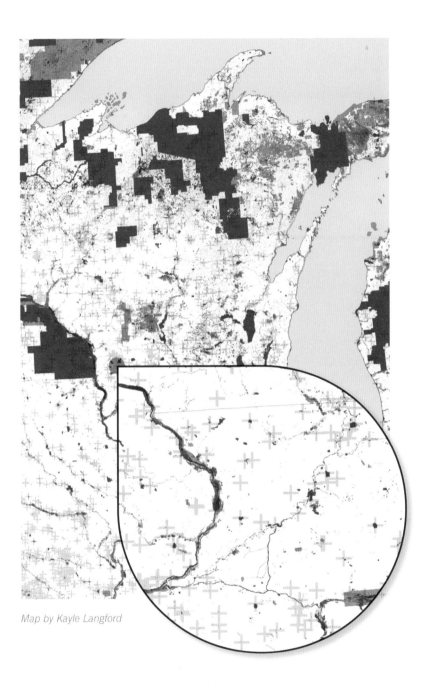

Map by Kayle Langford

↑ CLUSTERS AND ZONES

This map of dams and water hydrography shows how clusters of dams make a territory. Choosing a cross-style mapping mark allows for a geography zone to be read without masking significant map details.

NOTES ON:

LINES AND MARKERS

To bring focus to a map, lines need to have layers of hierarchy. Their weight, layer sequence and color can impact the way they are read.

Clusters of points can operate as a field, making a territory from singular, discrete elements.

HIERARCHY AND DETAIL

COLOR, TOO, COMMUNICATES INFORMATION. Just as with line weights and other mark techniques, color can enhance the way information is read and understood. Thinking about color as a tool, rather than a label, strengthens relationships between components.

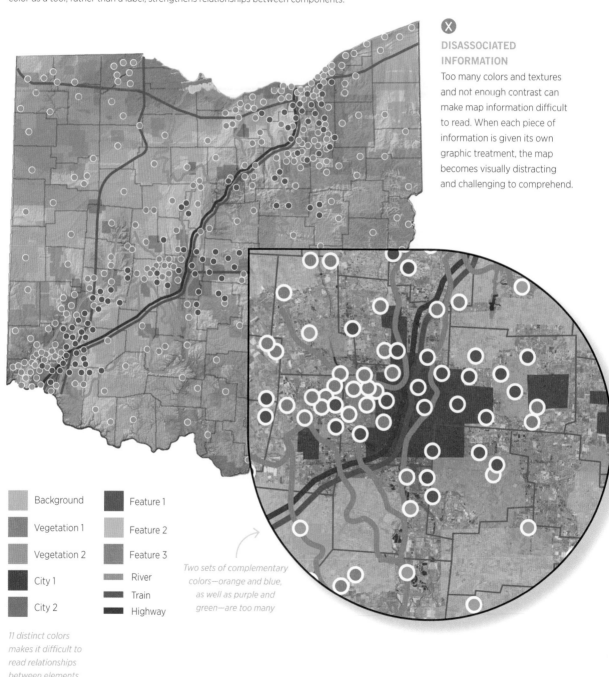

⊗ DISASSOCIATED INFORMATION

Too many colors and textures and not enough contrast can make map information difficult to read. When each piece of information is given its own graphic treatment, the map becomes visually distracting and challenging to comprehend.

Background	Feature 1
Vegetation 1	Feature 2
Vegetation 2	Feature 3
City 1	River
City 2	Train
	Highway

Two sets of complementary colors—orange and blue, as well as purple and green—are too many

11 distinct colors makes it difficult to read relationships between elements

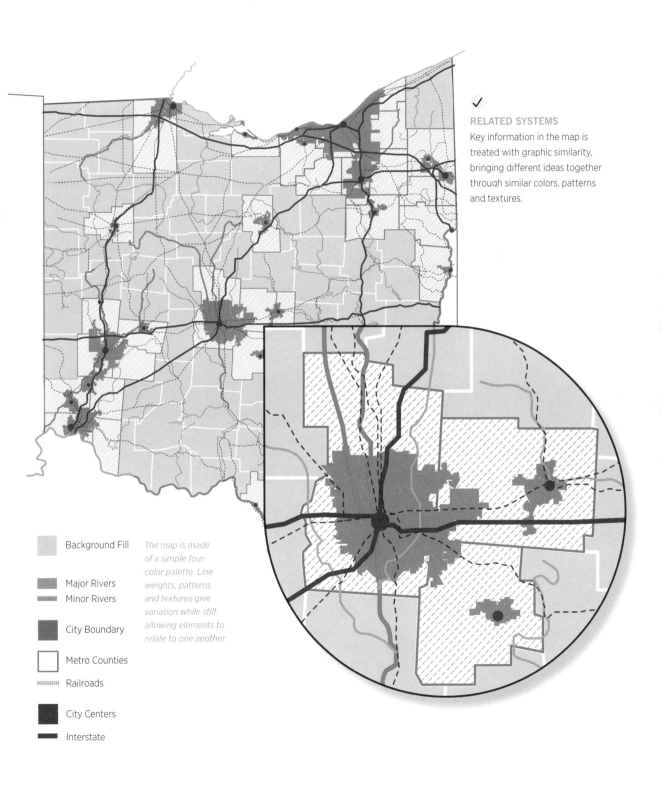

✓

RELATED SYSTEMS
Key information in the map is
treated with graphic similarity,
bringing different ideas together
through similar colors, patterns
and textures.

Background Fill

Major Rivers

Minor Rivers

City Boundary

Metro Counties

Railroads

City Centers

Interstate

*The map is made
of a simple four-
color palette. Line
weights, patterns
and textures give
variation while still
allowing elements to
relate to one another*

NICHOLAS FELTON

GRAPHIC DESIGNER / NEW YORK, NY

THE FELTRON 2008 ATLAS

MICHAEL POLLAN LECTURE · FIRST HOCKEY GAME · BEAT GRAND THEFT AUTO · FIRST ICE CREAM OF SUMMER · SECRET SERVICE VISITS OFFICE · OBAMA ELECTED · AMADOR'S APPENDIX REMOVED

NICHOLAS FELTON *is a graphic and information designer who spends much of his time thinking about data, charts and our daily routines. He is the author of several* Personal Annual Reports *that weave numerous measurements into a tapestry of graphs, maps and statistics that reflect the year's activities. He is the co-founder of Daytum.com and currently a member of the product design team at Facebook. His work has been profiled in publications including the* Wall Street Journal, Wired *and* Good Magazine *and he has been recognized as one of the 50 most influential designers in America by* Fast Company.

GRAPHIC DESIGN FOR ARCHITECTS:
You're a graphic designer deeply interested in space. How do you use space as a tool for developing your work?

NICHOLAS FELTON: One of the things I look for in my practice are aspects of behavior that are universally relatable—space, miles traveled, categories of places visited, all of these things are undeniable aspects of people's behavior. They form these touch points between me and my readers. One of these things this project tries to do is act like a mirror for the reader. It's not so much about "I went to the bar this many times" but rather "I went this many times, how many did *you* go?" or

"I spent this many hours at home, how many hours did *you* spend at home?" In this respect, space is a channel for communicating and connecting with other people.

GDA: How do you relate that idea of location to more contemporary ways of connecting with others through mobile devices or other technologies. Is the future placeless?

NF: Placeless is interesting, it's pervasive. For example, Facebook is in as many spaces as I am. I've spent a lot of time at Facebook thinking about the value of place. It's revealing to see a map of all of

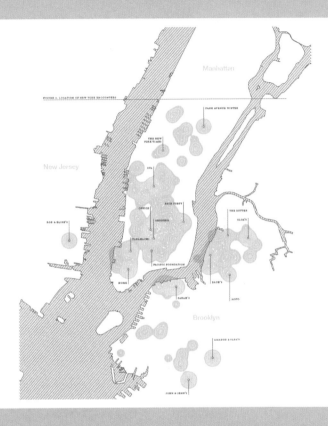

Distribution

Date and location of encounters.

FIGURE 1. —— ENCOUNTERS / —— RESPONSES

JAN
HONG KONG
FEB
WILLINGTON
MAR
AUSTIN   OKLAHOMA CITY BOSTON
APR
BELFAST
MAY
MILL VALLEY
JUN
JUL
D.C.   BELMAR
AUG
ALEXANDRIA
SEP
OCT
CAMDEN
NOV
DEC
D.C.   MILL VALLEY

METHODOLOGY

Throughout 2009, friends, family, co-workers and acquaintances of Nicholas Felton were asked to report on his activities whenever they met.

All data on the following pages was compiled from the responses of these participants to a variety of questions concerning their encounter.

FIGURE 2. LOCATION OF NEW YORK ENCOUNTERS

TOTAL ENCOUNTERS	**AVERAGE ENCOUNTERS PER DAY**	**SURVEYS COMPLETED**	**CUMULATIVE RESPONSE RATE**
1,761	4.8	560	32%
COUNTRIES INVOLVED	**STATES INVOLVED**	**DAYS WITH REPORTS**	**CONTRIBUTORS**
Three	Nine	254	210
U.S.A., HONG KONG AND NORTHERN IRELAND	CALIFORNIA, MAINE, MASSACHUSETTS, NEW JERSEY, NEW YORK, OKLAHOMA, TEXAS, VERMONT, VIRGINIA, PLUS WASHINGTON D.C.	70% OF THE YEAR	AVERAGE 2.66 REPORTS PER PERSON

the places where you've checked in. When working at Facebook, we realized that privacy through obscurity has dissolved. If something is visible in the system, then you see it, other people see it. On the other hand, if you don't want it to be seen, then you have controls for hiding. The map was an interesting part of that dynamic. If you have created all of these check-ins, you have created a dataset of information that now exists. You created it. If you don't want anyone to know you went to Japan, then don't show anyone you went to Japan. Remove it from your dataset. Or if you want to share that experience, there's a platform for sharing that information. The map becomes a record of the data about your life.

GDA: You're crafting information from a "dataset" formed by your personal experiences. In your work, you choose to show this information through maps or information graphics. Why those means? Why not photos or text?

NF: All of these topics are about trying to deal with your dataset. In any system you have oldest to newest, largest to smallest, here to there. How do you organize and sort this information? In terms of organizing principles, space is a fascinating one. I've been thinking about photos a lot lately. For example, I'm trying to show the whole expanse of the dataset, instead of just an interesting corner of it or one discrete piece of it. So

↑ **MAPPING INFORMATION**

Nicholas Felton's Annual Reports combine different datasets and are visualized through maps, diagrams, charts and other information graphics. (above left) The Feltron 2008 Annual Report Poster (above right) The Feltron 2009 Annual Report.

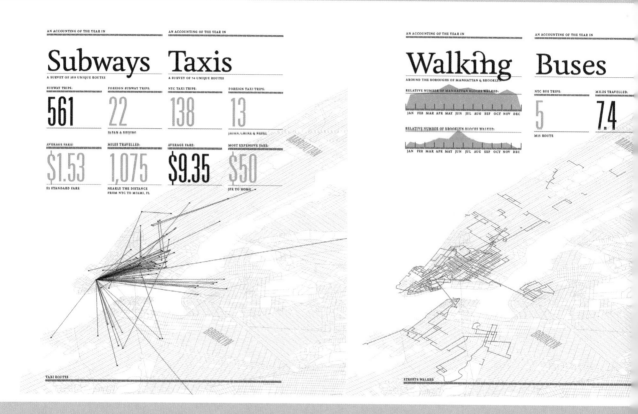

AN ACCOUNTING OF THE YEAR IN

Subways Taxis

A SURVEY OF 109 UNIQUE ROUTES   A SURVEY OF 74 UNIQUE ROUTES

SUBWAY TRIPS:	FOREIGN SUBWAY TRIPS:	NYC TAXI TRIPS:	FOREIGN TAXI TRIPS:
561	22	138	13
	JAPAN & BEIJING		JAPAN, CHINA & NEPAL

AVERAGE FARE:	MILES TRAVELLED:	AVERAGE FARE:	MOST EXPENSIVE FARE:
$1.53	1,075	**$9.35**	$50
$2 STANDARD FARE	NEARLY THE DISTANCE FROM NYC TO MIAMI, FL		JFK TO HOME

TAXI ROUTES

AN ACCOUNTING OF THE YEAR IN

Walking Buses

AROUND THE BOROUGHS OF MANHATTAN & BROOKLYN

RELATIVE NUMBER OF MANHATTAN BLOCKS WALKED:

JAN FEB MAR APR MAY JUN JUL AUG SEP OCT NOV DEC

RELATIVE NUMBER OF BROOKLYN BLOCKS WALKED:

JAN FEB MAR APR MAY JUN JUL AUG SEP OCT NOV DEC

NYC BUS TRIPS:	MILES TRAVELLED:
5	**7.4**
M15 ROUTE	

STREETS WALKED

---

the photography page, I could encompass the whole dataset by stating the number of photos taken: 5,000. I could make a purposeful selection, such as the first one and the last one. Or I could show all of the photos taken at a specific hour. It's much harder to show just all of the photos because they are much more information-dense. And it would be very difficult to do on only one page. Now that we have so many more photos, it's an interesting problem to try to develop aggregate representation tools. How do you show the breadth and depth of your photos? There are some tools that do this—Facebook and Instagram use maps that tag your photos so you can view your images through geography. Without that tool, you just look

at your photos as a single chronology.

There's a new project that's dealing with this problem by taking photos every three minutes. But how do you find the meaning in this? Photos are very robust, but we need to talk about them not just as data points but as problems of aggregation. For example, you end the day with 1,500 photos. An obvious aggregate solution is to make a time lapse of the photos, but that doesn't relate to print. What are the other solutions? Long exposure is one technique. When the new MoMA was built, they installed a camera that filmed the construction over three or four years.

I wonder how technology can fit into these questions. It's the aggregate problems that I'm interested in solving.

GDA: You've been testing different ways of representing information and sharing these data collection methods through your *Annual Reports*. How has this project grown to become a longer project based in your questions about aggregation?

NF: After I graduated with my Graphic Design degree from RISD, I worked in New York for many years, and I was always making personal projects for my website. Travel exhibitions, typeface designs. I was just looking for graphic fodder, for things that connected with me and connected with an audience. One year I wanted to do a retrospective for the end of the year and, as I started to dig I found places where I had left behind data that I could extract.

I'm a music lover and I'd been using Last. FM, a website that had been tracking all of my music listens. I had taken fairly accurate calendar records of where I went out to eat. Photographs were information-rich, too. That first annual report was a project that resonated, bloggers picked it up and strangers emailed me saying "This is awesome! I want to make an annual report of my life!" After that I thought I would do a print thing, so I wanted to be more deliberate and track for it. The project has been a symbiotic thing with my audience and where the internet continues to be encouraging. It hasn't said "We've had enough, stop now." At the moment I keep having new ideas—I know what this year's *Annual Report* will be, I know what next year's is going to be. After that it will be ten years and I might finish the project then. I have an obsession with keeping dates and times to neat integers. I left Facebook two years to the day that I started. Maybe after these ten years I will compile all of the *Annual Reports* into a book.

GDA: How have the reports evolved since you began them?

NF: There are a couple of evolutions happening. The reports are now themed and there is a central thesis to each one. 2010, for example, was about my father's life. In 2011 I condensed those two years together so there is a visual interplay between the datasets. Another one is about

↑ **PERSONAL NARRATIVES**

(Above left) The Feltron 2007 Annual Report; *(above right)* The Feltron 2010 Annual Report. *(above far right) detail from the* 2010 Report

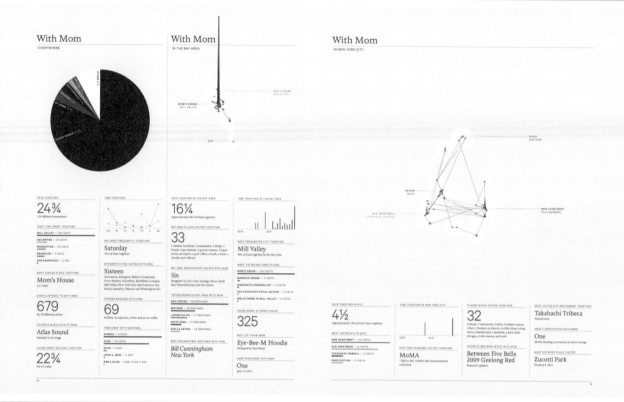

sampling methods—different reports. Eliminating caring about completeness and just focusing on the momentary stuff. So graphically I think they're getting a little bit esoteric. I picked up Processing in 2009 and have become more familiar with the code. Before this, all of the collecting was by hand, the dataset wasn't large. So all of it then was about bringing specificity, typographic rigor to these forms, making a nicely designed pie chart. Now there's so much more data, there's so many more people working with it trying to make it easily consumable.

I've moved on from making it more digestible. My focus is still on trying to make interesting stories and a product that's easy to read. But a lot of the forms that I'm using are a bit harder to approach.

It's kind of how I've come full-circle. I had started out by working against some of the computer-generating information tools that were hard to interface with, but now that I have some of those technical abilities I'm making network graphs, which are not the easiest things to consume. But I'm putting my own critique on them and try to make information from them that is meaningful.

GDA: It's still curation—no matter what the tools you have to gather and analyze the data, you have to design its output. How do you craft these decisions?

NF: You have to know what controls to put on it. Without these controls, many of these diagrams are a mess, spaghetti and meatballs. When you put some controls

on it, you can set the threshold. You can decide if you have a solid or not, or how many connections yields a particular scale. It's interesting to have these dynamic tools now for visual experiments. Before you were working manually with composition, and that composition is still there, but it's no longer graphic design techniques. It's the intersection of graphics and computer science.

GDA: How do you see data changing? How is the representation of information going to change our lives?

NF: I'm not sure if it's having a fundamental effect on society. But it's definitely a new material that is in society. Everything is instrumented, or will be

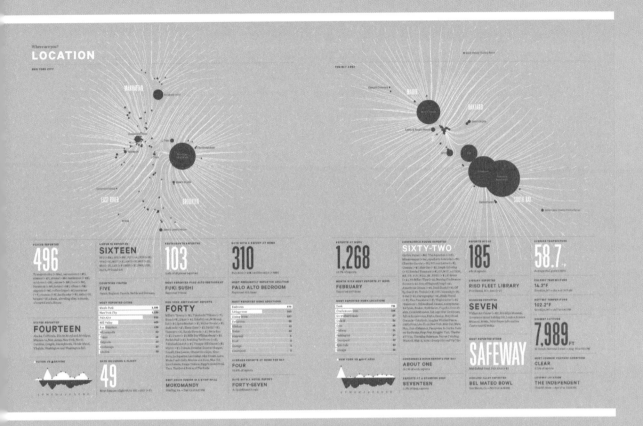

instrumented. You name it, there's a data source for it. It doesn't exist now, but it's something that someone is taking advantage of. For example, I don't have great access for the dataset for my car, but by the end of the year I'll have something that I can plug into my car and collect information about my car, and the places my car interfaces.

There's a lot of additional material in the world and you need tools and techniques to make sense of it. You have a relationship to your car, to your phone, to people, to your government. All of these will be open pathways to you and you have to decide what you want to do with that data. And to clamor for opening the relationships that aren't currently available. I think the more pathways we have, the more of a

requirement there will be for people to have the tools to understand this data. How to do simple mapping, simple graphing, give us ways of understanding this information?

GDA: How do we empower others to interface with data?

NF: We need better access, more tools, more literacy as well. There is the potential for changing the shape of people's lives, the shape of societies. Once you measure something, you can affect it.

↑ **PROCESSING**

(Above left) The Feltron 2011 Annual Report; *(above right)* The Feltron 2012 Annual Report. *Graphs are made using the programming tool Processing.*

COMMUNICATION AS ARCHITECTURE

SIGNAGE

CLARIFYING EXPERIENCE

SIGNAGE IS THE INTERFACE BETWEEN ARCHITECTURE AND ITS USER.
Whether it be the space of a complicated building, or clarifying the interaction
between the subway and the rider, signage serves to help the user navigate space.

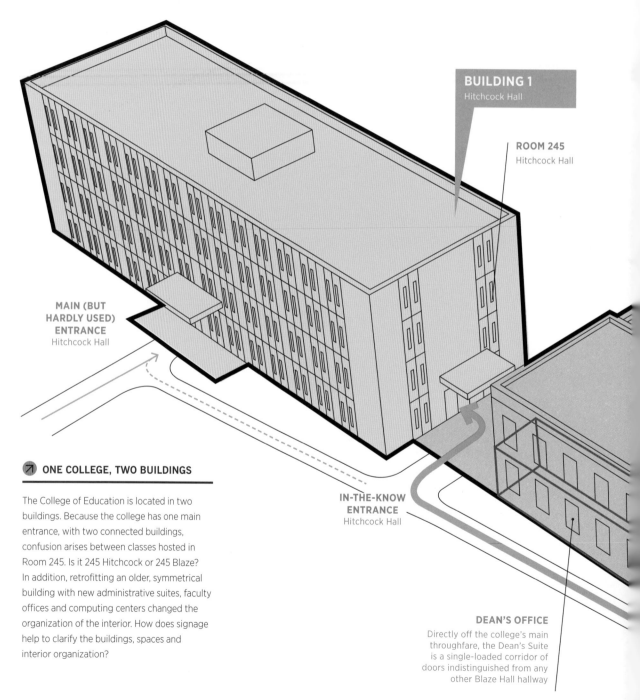

BUILDING 1
Hitchcock Hall

ROOM 245
Hitchcock Hall

**MAIN (BUT
HARDLY USED)
ENTRANCE**
Hitchcock Hall

**IN-THE-KNOW
ENTRANCE**
Hitchcock Hall

↗ ONE COLLEGE, TWO BUILDINGS

The College of Education is located in two
buildings. Because the college has one main
entrance, with two connected buildings,
confusion arises between classes hosted in
Room 245. Is it 245 Hitchcock or 245 Blaze?
In addition, retrofitting an older, symmetrical
building with new administrative suites, faculty
offices and computing centers changed the
organization of the interior. How does signage
help to clarify the buildings, spaces and
interior organization?

DEAN'S OFFICE
Directly off the college's main
throughfare, the Dean's Suite
is a single-loaded corridor of
doors indistinguished from any
other Blaze Hall hallway

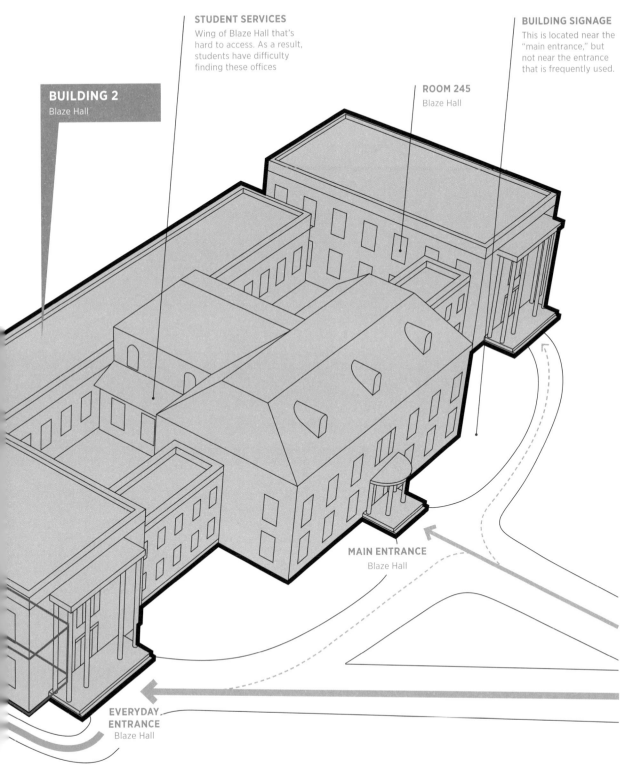

STUDENT SERVICES
Wing of Blaze Hall that's hard to access. As a result, students have difficulty finding these offices

BUILDING SIGNAGE
This is located near the "main entrance," but not near the entrance that is frequently used.

BUILDING 2
Blaze Hall

ROOM 245
Blaze Hall

MAIN ENTRANCE
Blaze Hall

EVERYDAY ENTRANCE
Blaze Hall

SIGNAGE SYSTEMS

SIGNAGE IS A GRAPHIC STANDARD FOR NAVIGATION. How you communicate building information is part of the visual standards that inform architectural space. How the signage orients and organizes the visitor should be part of the architecture's intention.

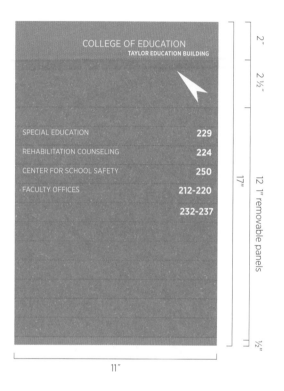

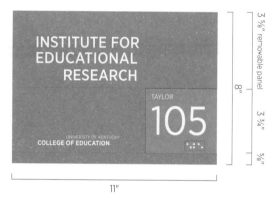

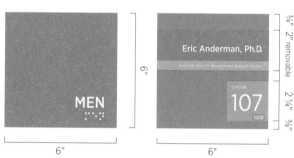

CHANGING SPACES

The college comprises two distinct yet connected buildings. To help clarify the spaces of one building over another, two color systems are used. One building is coded in orange signage while the other uses blue signage. The contrast gives visual difference to the two buildings, while still maintaining a singular college identity.

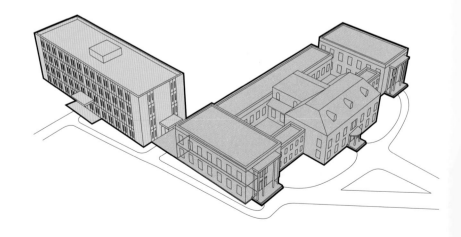

NOTES ON:

COLOR CONTRAST

Signs that contain visual characters must have a high dark-to-light (or light-to-dark) contrast between characters and their background in order for them to be compliant. The important issue is not a specific color, but rather the contrast produced between lightness and darkness.

Good contrast

Not enough

Not great, but passable

SPATIAL RELATIONSHIPS

LIKE ARCHITECTURE, SIGNAGE HAS TO ADHERE TO PUBLIC CODES. Having a basic grasp of these relationships can allow for codes to be followed while allowing room for spatial invention. Laws vary between states so be sure to consult local regulations.

PERMANENT ROOM SIGNS

Permanent rooms such as restrooms, exits and rooms numbers all must comply with code standards.

Character Style:
- Sans serif typeface
- All capital letters

Signage Finish:
- Characters and background will have a non-glare finish

Contrast:
- Characters and pictograms must contrast with the background color

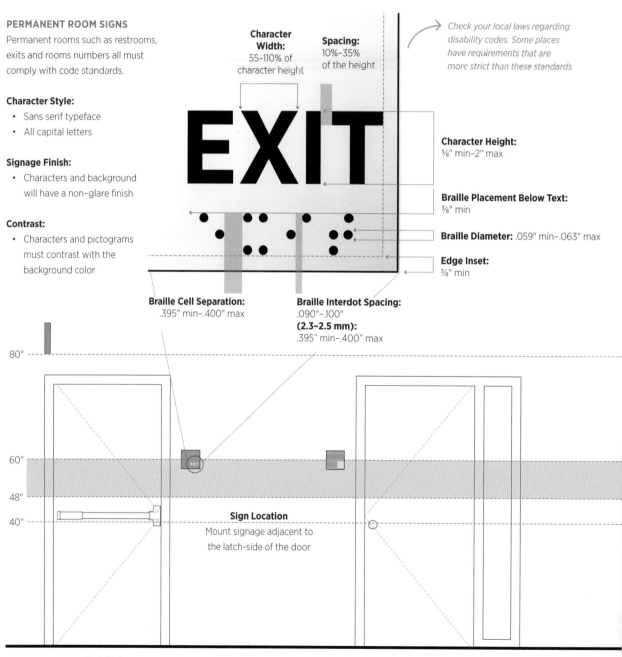

Character Width:
55–110% of character height

Spacing:
10%–35% of the height

Check your local laws regarding disability codes. Some places have requirements that are more strict than these standards

Character Height:
⅝" min–2" max

Braille Placement Below Text:
⅜" min

Braille Diameter: .059" min–.063" max

Edge Inset:
⅜" min

Braille Cell Separation:
.395" min–.400" max

Braille Interdot Spacing:
.090"–.100"
(2.3–2.5 mm):
.395" min–.400" max

80"

60"

48"

40"

Sign Location
Mount signage adjacent to the latch-side of the door

Exit Stair

Individual Office

Line Spacing:
⅝" min — 2" max

TEMPORARY INFORMATION SIGNS

Building directories, menus or signs that provide temporary information, such as a current occupant's name, only need to adhere to visual guidelines. Tactile guides are not required for these signs.

Semi-permanent Spaces:

- Offices
- Classrooms
- Multi-use rooms

Character Style:

- Sans serif and serif typeface
- Capital, lowercase

Signage Finish:

- Same as permanent

Contrast:

- Same as permanent

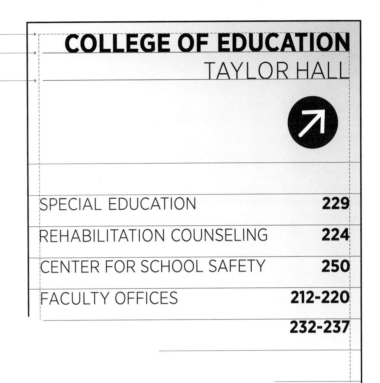

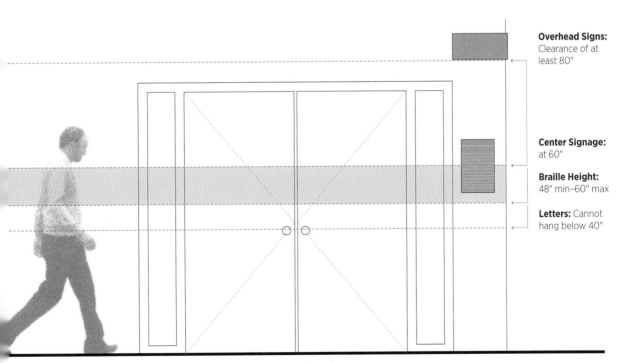

Overhead Signs:
Clearance of at least 80"

Center Signage:
at 60"

Braille Height:
48" min–60" max

Letters: Cannot hang below 40"

Administrative Suite

SURFACES COMMUNICATE

SIGNAGE ISN'T AN ADDITIONAL GRAPHIC, IT IS A WAY OF STRUCTURING SPACE.

How you set up the logic of this piece of paper addresses – want to say something about how the page structures and organizes content.

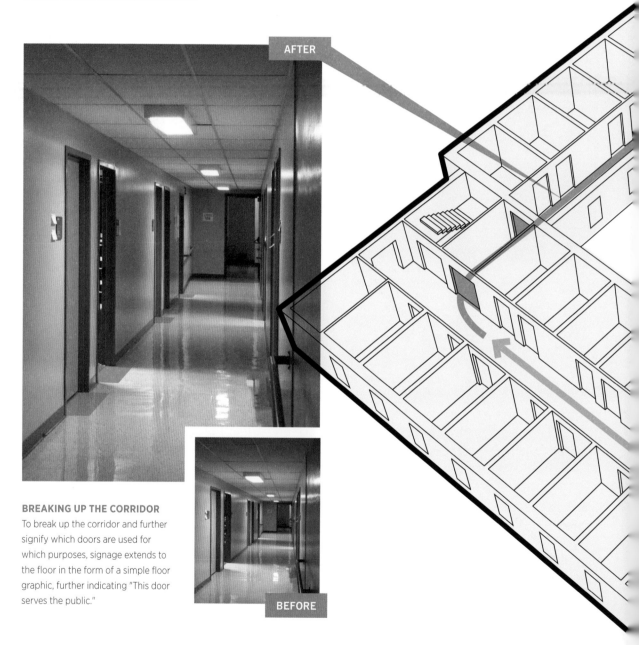

AFTER

BEFORE

BREAKING UP THE CORRIDOR
To break up the corridor and further signify which doors are used for which purposes, signage extends to the floor in the form of a simple floor graphic, further indicating "This door serves the public."

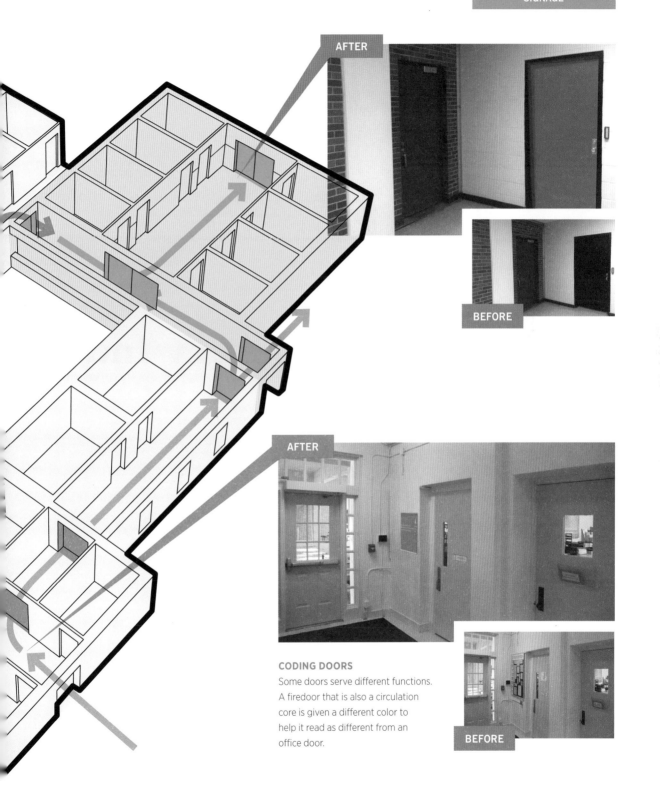

AFTER

BEFORE

AFTER

CODING DOORS
Some doors serve different functions.
A firedoor that is also a circulation
core is given a different color to
help it read as different from an
office door.

BEFORE

LARGE-SCALE LEGIBILITY

TYPOGRAPHY HAS DYNAMIC RELATIONSHIPS. Proportions at one scale can look different at another. When changing scale from print to a building, for example, new issues arise. Paying attention to these relationships can help text maintain its legibility.

KERNING

Kerning is the process of adjusting the spacing between individual letters, while tracking (letter spacing) adjusts spacing uniformly over the entire word. In a well-kerned word the two-dimensional blank spaces between each pair of characters all have similar area.

Tracking

Before, no kerning

After, with kerning

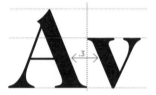 

NO KERNING
The edges of the A and V line up without any overlap. A wide gap is created between the letters.

KERNING
The edges of the A and V overlap to form a tighter relationship.

SAME TRACKING, DIFFERENT KERNING
While tracking between the top and bottom examples is the same, the kerning on the bottom demonstrates proportional letter spacing.

TRACKING

Tracking adjusts spacing uniformly over the entire word.

Before, only tracking

**WIDE TRACKING,
NO KERNING**
As spaces between letters get larger, it's easier to see uneven spaces between letters.

After, tracking and kerning

**WIDE TRACKING,
AND KERNING**
Kerning becomes more noticeable, and significant to legibility, when letters change scale.

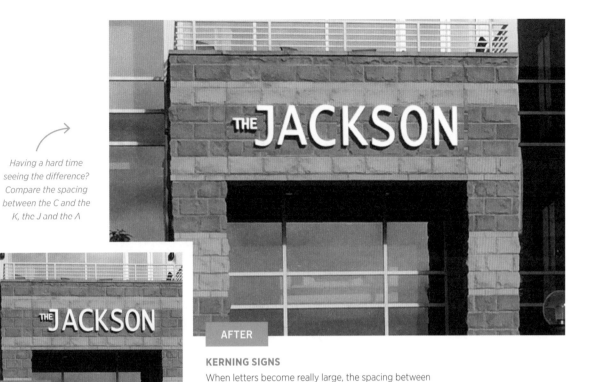

Having a hard time seeing the difference? Compare the spacing between the C and the K, the J and the A

AFTER

BEFORE

KERNING SIGNS

When letters become really large, the spacing between them become even more critical. To the untrained eye, kerning is a subtle practice, but makes architectural signage more graceful and legible. When done well, you won't even notice proper kerning.

WRONG

 TOP DOWN

RIGHT

✓ **STRAIGHT ACROSS**

LEFT IS RIGHT

It's a common mistake to design blade signage with English letters stacked on top of one another. English characters should be typeset as they are read—left to right, rather than top to bottom.

LANDSCAPE SIGNAGE

ENVIRONMENTAL SIGNAGE IS A MATERIAL AND SPATIAL PROJECT. Developing navigation sited within the complexity of the world, versus the control of a building, requires a deep awareness of space and structure.

Brooklyn Bridge Park
Open

FROM A DISTANCE
How does signage operate within the visual chaos of a busy urban park? Large surfaces and saturated colors complement the park setting while remaining legible.

Brooklyn Bridge Park
Open

MATERIAL ICONS

Programmatic spaces are clarified with activity icons, added well above eye level on concrete piers. The icons integrate the material language of the park with its programming.

OPEN

SCOTT STOWELL, PROPRIETOR / NEW YORK, NY

①

SCOTT STOWELL *is the proprietor of Open, an independent design studio that creates rewarding experiences for people who look, read and think. Open projects include identity systems for Bravo and New York Public Radio, editorial design for* Good *magazine and Stanford's d.school, short films for Jazz at Lincoln Center and* Time *magazine, architectural signage for Brooklyn Bridge Park and Yale University, and integrated campaigns for Google and Patagonia.*

GRAPHIC DESIGN FOR ARCHITECTS: In your work, how do graphic design and architecture intersect?

SCOTT STOWELL: The simplest answer is that we sometimes work with architects, and we know things that they don't and they know things that we don't. We have experience designing signage, and even within graphic design that's a highly specialized field. Architects have to worry about health and safety issues, and we have signage guidelines enforced by the Americans with Disabilities Act. This is all practical stuff, governed by codes and laws and rules.

In designing signage that works with architecture, though, I'm always interested in creating rewarding experiences for people. When architects engage a graphic designer to do that work, they want to work with somebody who can make choices that have meaning. So the work we like to do always has some ideas behind it, but I don't want people to have to know about those ideas in order to experience or enjoy the work.

GDA: What were the ideas driving the signage project you did for the Yale University Art Gallery?

SS: The work we did for the Yale Art Gallery was our first signage project. It's in a pretty impressive building by Louis Kahn. Actually, it's the first building he did that really looks like a "Louis Kahn" building. The

Gallery's mission is that the place should be free and open to all. You don't need to be affiliated with Yale; you don't need to pay admission; you can just walk in and visit. Our goal with the signage was to fulfill that mission of openness and also respect the physical architecture of the Kahn building.

The material choices we selected made the signage some of the most expensive work we've ever commissioned. When we interviewed for the project, we researched tons of other museum signage systems. We found out most room signs are made out of plastic and stuck on the wall with double-stick tape. But this is a Louis Kahn building! The signage couldn't be plastic. It needed to be made of real stuff, and that stuff needed to have integrity, in the same way Kahn thought about materials in the building. So instead of gluing plastic letters on the front of metal plaques, we had zinc plates made and processed in an acid bath, so the letters are integral to the material. Every room sign is what it looks like: one solid piece of metal.

Of course this was kind of hard to get made. Originally, we wanted to just leave the metal as it was when it came out of the acid bath (we finally had to paint the surface, but we used a gray that matched one Kahn used elsewhere in the building). Manufacturers kept trying to fake it by roughing up cheap metal to look "artsy," as one of them called it. But we wanted the material to be real—to reveal the actual processes used, not just represent them. The room signs are screw-mounted into the building mortar. At first our manufacturer glued sawed-off screw heads onto the front of the sign. We said, "No. We want those to be the screws. Literally, the screws holding it up are the screws you see." This took a while.

GDA: In your practice, do you often think about materiality?

SS: We think about ink on paper. We think about pixels on a screen. We think about metal and stone. What's the difference? You have a thing to design and you make decisions based on what you want to do. Everything is always a different material,

so we don't see material as an element that changes the way we design. Material is part of the process like anything else. We're always doing the same design work. We just use different materials.

The theories behind Kahn's work could never register to a regular person coming to visit the architecture. They shouldn't have to, anyway! It's the same with our signage. How can we enhance the visual experience of this building? There's a lot of wayfinding in the world that is just that: "Bathroom this way." I'm sure it looks fine, has nice colors and follows ADA rules, but what about being part of someone's visual experience? The person coming to see the museum's collection needs to be able to function in the building, but the signage should be part of the aesthetic experience of the entire museum.

In all of our work, I always want to find the balancing point: the intersection where as many different people can relate to the work as possible. The Yale signage had to look right, feel right and work right, but it had to have ideas guiding the design. Ideas help guide design choices. Because when you're faced with every choice possible, what's the most meaningful decision you can make in that moment?

GDA: Your signage projects always seem so effortless, so integrated into the spaces they occupy.

SS: We try to work with abstract systems that anyone can understand, but simplicity isn't simple to make. With the Yale project, there were a lot of dead ends along the way. At the end, the simplicity of the signage was very hard to get to.

We were invited by ARO (Architecture Research Office) to do the signage for the Friedman Study Center in the Sciences Library at Brown University. Their project had a very small budget—they were basically replacing the furniture to make the place more comfortable for students. The Center is open 24 hours a day and is full of spaces where you can work and hang out. It's on the bottom three floors of a super modern 1960s concrete tower. I think every college campus has one of these. It was also already filled with old signage from the 1960s. So we decided to embrace that look of the future from the past, as seen in movies like *2001*.

We wanted to mark the actual building—to allow the signage to be in contact with the building materials. We wanted to tag the building rather than sign the building. So we came up with the idea of silkscreening images and text from the

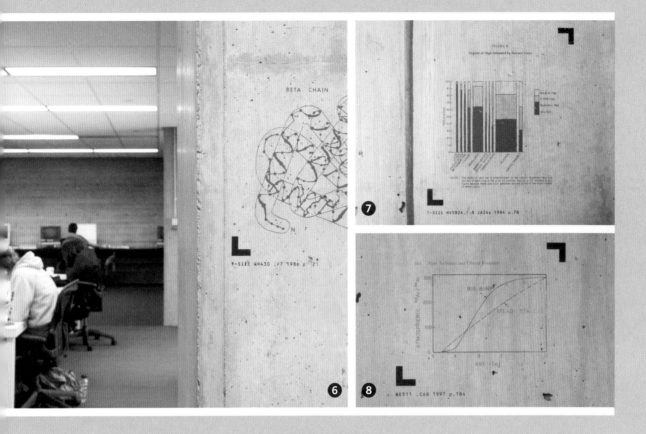

library collections on the walls. We put out a call to faculty, staff and students asking them to email us ideas from books in the library. The librarians were really into it! We added these images all over the Center.

My favorites are in weird places, like when we would move a filing cabinet, put an image behind it, and then move the cabinet back. I love knowing that image won't be discovered until they move the furniture in a few years. Remember, this is a place where students work day and night, pull all-nighters, eat pizza and sleep. We wanted to celebrate the culture of the place—to make the space memorable, not just functional.

For this project the silkscreeners we worked with were amazing. The interior walls of that space are board-formed concrete, so some have wood textures and others have very smooth surfaces.

The silkscreeners only had one shot to do the screening and every time they were perfect. There was some retouching with paintbrushes, but in general it was a successful and pretty inexpensive process. By adding these elements along with the regular room signs, we made the idea a part of the building, not just some signs in the building.

GDA: It seems like your work is based in imaginative ways of integrating into the environment, but with playful pragmatism.

SS: Every choice we make is a design decision. Under these circumstances, at this time, with this budget, you make the best series of choices you can—as long as you have space in your head to think clearly.

↑ **MATERIAL INTEGRATION**

1–3: Yale University Art Gallery, New Haven, CT

4–8: Friedman Study Center, Sciences Library, Brown University, Providence, RI

4–5: *The project expands the building's vernacular 1960s graphic quality.*

6–8: *Silk-screened images from the library's holdings reflect the Center's visual culture.*

COMMUNICATION AS ARCHITECTURE

SUPERGRAPHICS

WHAT MAKES THEM SUPER?

ORIGINALLY COMPRISED OF A PALETTE OF ARROWS, LINES AND WORDS applied with paint, contemporary supergraphics engage many new technologies. Supergraphics are a spatial tool to engage architecture surfaces, be they interior walls, building facades or urban spaces. When images become this large, they cross the line into architectural surface.

Flower-print facade is made from porcelain and steel panels

SUPERGRAPHIC AS DISGUISE

Best Stores, Venturi Scott Brown

Supergraphics are used to disguise the facades of the big box department store. The graphic has no relation to programmatic function and instead explores the aesthetic function of architecture within the rise of suburban retail development.

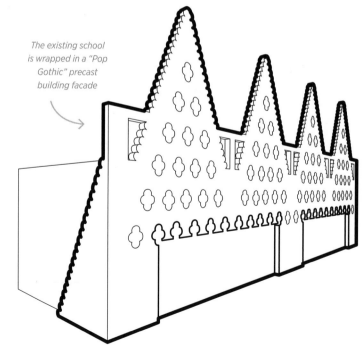

The existing school is wrapped in a "Pop Gothic" precast building facade

SUPERGRAPHIC AS IDENTITY

Sint Lucas, Fashion Architecture Taste

Unremarkable existing buildings are given a lively new identity with a thickened architectural surface. A "strong, colourful and unusual new external identity [is developed] through the addition of decorative screens, surface treatments and signage."

READING LIST:

SUPER GRAPHICS

Charles Jencks
The Language of Post-Modern Architecture Rizzoli (1977)

Robert Venturi, Steven Izenour and Denise Scott Brown
Learning from Las Vegas: The Forgotten Symbolism of Architectural Form MIT Press (1977)

Charles Jencks, Sean Griffiths, Charles Holland and Sam Jacob
Radical Post-Modernism: Architectural Design Wiley (2011)

Michael Rock
Multiple Signatures Rizzoli (2013)

John McMorrough
"Blowing the Lid off Paint" in
Hunch 11: Rethinking Representation
Berlage Institut (2006)

Per Mollerup
Wayshowing > Wayfinding: Basic & Interactive
BIS Publishers (2013)

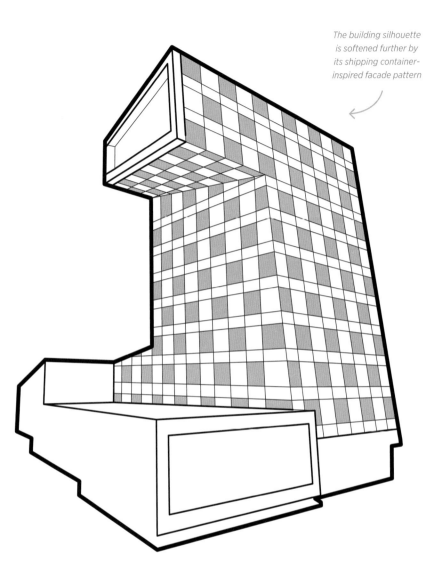

The building silhouette is softened further by its shipping container-inspired facade pattern

SUPERGRAPHIC AS CONTEXT
Shipping and Transport College, Neutelings Riedijk

The graphic facade links the building form back to its location along near the industrial port on the Maas River, making a robust volume an emblematic icon for the college by referring to the sculptural harbour architecture of silos, cranes and walls of stacked shipping containers. It draws an unbroken industrial skin over the building form to further emphasize the maritime character of the building.

CONCEALING THE SURFACE

SUPERGRAPHICS OF THE 1970S explored the relationship between perception and context. A bright stripe could situate disparate pieces of architectural detris (radiators, light switches, fire extinguishers) or develop new spatial constructions by playing with perspective.

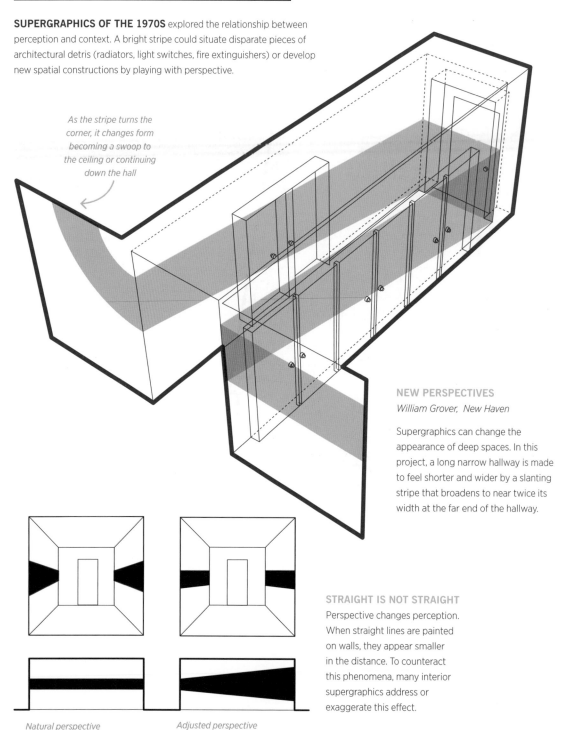

As the stripe turns the corner, it changes form becoming a swoop to the ceiling or continuing down the hall

NEW PERSPECTIVES
William Grover, New Haven

Supergraphics can change the appearance of deep spaces. In this project, a long narrow hallway is made to feel shorter and wider by a slanting stripe that broadens to near twice its width at the far end of the hallway.

Natural perspective

Adjusted perspective

STRAIGHT IS NOT STRAIGHT
Perspective changes perception. When straight lines are painted on walls, they appear smaller in the distance. To counteract this phenomena, many interior supergraphics address or exaggerate this effect.

"Supergraphics is a magnificent device for playing with scale. They make a toy out of a room."
—Charles Moore

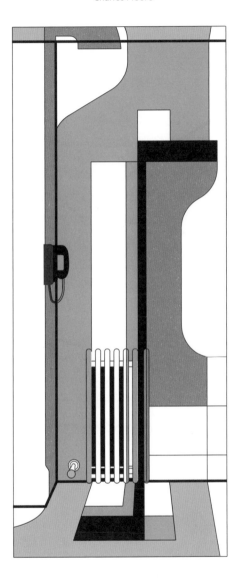

Illinois Institute of Technology
McCormick Student Center
2x4

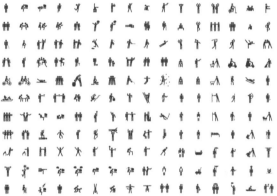

SUPERGRAPHIC AS MESSAGE

Illinois Institute of Technology
McCormick Tribune Campus Center, OMA / 2x4

The building graphics embrace the collegiate experience through an exuberant system of icons depicting typical and imagined student activities. Integrated throughout the building in many ways, the icons themselves form images of IIT's iconic architectural figure, Mies van der Rohe.

SUPERGRAPHIC AS DISGUISE

New Haven Office, Charles Moore

The inherent graphic of the radiator extends to the surrounding architecture, creating a playful context for the inclusion of necessary infrastructural components.

SUPERGRAPHIC AS BRAND

GRAPHICS PROJECT IDENTITY. When scaled to the building facade, text, logos or other patterns broadcast an abstracted corporate message. Oftentimes the brand projected onto the building facade is entirely independent of the architecture's program, serving as a further layer of corporate identity.

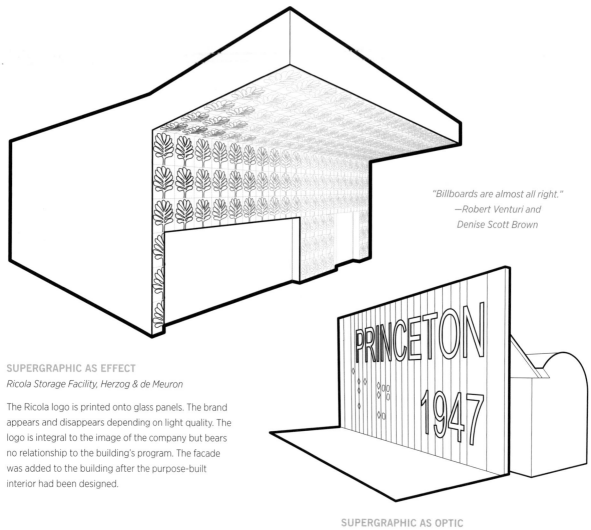

"Billboards are almost all right."
—Robert Venturi and
Denise Scott Brown

SUPERGRAPHIC AS EFFECT
Ricola Storage Facility, Herzog & de Meuron

The Ricola logo is printed onto glass panels. The brand appears and disappears depending on light quality. The logo is integral to the image of the company but bears no relationship to the building's program. The facade was added to the building after the purpose-built interior had been designed.

SUPERGRAPHIC AS OPTIC
National College Football Hall of Fame,
Venturi, Rauch and Scott Brown

The "Bill-Ding-Board" emphasizes communication as entertainment. The building provides images of football plays for public consumption, literally acting as a screen to display a combination of images and data—a first stab at an architecture for the sake of optics.

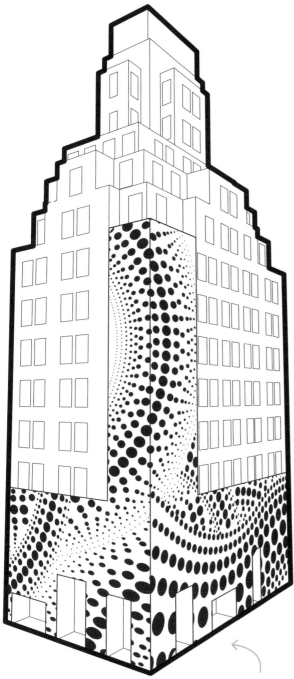

Artist Yayoi Kusama's swirling polkadot pattern is an exuberant layer wrapped over the steel-structure building

Louis Vuitton, Fifth Avenue, New York City

Louis Vuitton, Hong Kong

SUPER BRAND
Louis Vuitton Stores, various

Hyper-luxury brands explore the relationship between their logo and the environments they create. Louis Vuitton Stores expand their brand from their luggage to their building facade. By super-sizing their brand through an ever-changing group of artists and architects, Louis Vuitton also brands the street where their stores are located. Fifth Avenue is then branded with whatever pattern matches the current line of handbags.

URBAN SPACE GRAPHICS

GRAPHICS DON'T ALWAYS HAVE TO ADHERE TO THE WALL. Graphics located on the ground are also effective in transforming the character of a space. The urban ground is a place for graphics to have significant impact as they can direct movement, incorporate infrastructure and provide edges between programs.

SUPERGRAPHIC LANDSCAPE
Copacabana Beach, Rio de Janeiro, Roberto Burle Marx

For the hardscape edge of the beach, Burle Marx followed the distinctive paving patterns of the original walkways, which were covered in alternating black-and-white waves composed of small stones cut and laid by hand. This project demonstrates his ambition to elevate landscape design to the level of the fine arts.

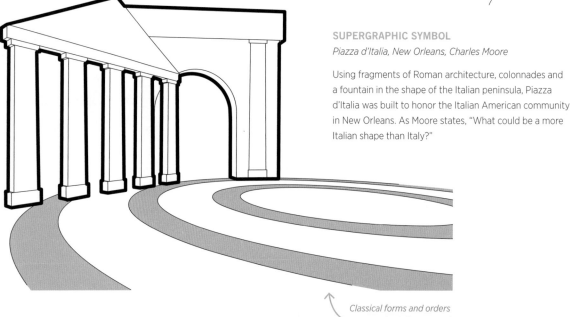

SUPERGRAPHIC SYMBOL
Piazza d'Italia, New Orleans, Charles Moore

Using fragments of Roman architecture, colonnades and a fountain in the shape of the Italian peninsula, Piazza d'Italia was built to honor the Italian American community in New Orleans. As Moore states, "What could be a more Italian shape than Italy?"

Classical forms and orders are playfully executed in modern materials

SUPERGRAPHIC GROUND

Franklin's Footpath, Gene Davis, Philadelphia

Gene Davis's 414-ft-long painting on the street in front of
the Philadelphia Museum of Art creates a dynamic urban
space leading to the museum. It changes the character of
the urban context by creating a vibrant, graphic ground
plane that leads directly to the art museum.

PROJECT PROJECTS

PREM KRISHNAMURTHY, PRINCIPAL / NEW YORK, NY

1

PREM KRISHNAMURTHY *is a founder and principal of Project Projects, a design studio focusing on print, identity, exhibition and interactive work with clients in art and architecture. Project Projects' clients include the Canadian Centre for Architecture, Field Operations, Guggenheim Museum, Harvard GSD, M+ Museum (Hong Kong), Michael Van Valkenburgh Associates, The Museum of Modern Art, New York City Department of Parks & Recreation, Phaidon, Princeton Architectural Press, SALT (Istanbul), Steven Holl Architects, Whitney Museum of American Art, WORKac and the Yale University Art Gallery.*

GRAPHIC DESIGN FOR ARCHITECTS: How does your practice intersect graphic design and architecture?

PREM KRISHNAMURTHY: We never set out to work specifically with architecture, but from the beginning of Project Projects those interests coalesced. Adam Michaels and I started the studio in 2004. We had nascent interests in architecture. I had studied graphic design, photography and fine art. Even in these other disciplines I was interested in volume, how people configured and occupied space.

In retrospect, that has a lot to do with why I'm interested in architecture, exhibition design and way-finding. Before starting Project Projects, Adam worked as

the Associate Art Director for *Architecture* magazine and had started his own practice designing architecture books. Adam and I started Project Projects with a shared interest in the field.

GDA: Describe further how you see graphic design as a spatial practice.

PK: I've always been interested in how graphics become real when they are located in space. There are some people who really like the way things look when they are abstractions; I like the way things look when they're physical. When you see them in the context of all the other junk in the world. There's so much visual information in this part of New York, for example, where

②

Chinatown meets the Lower East Side. Both of these neighborhoods are expanding so there's an interesting tension between the overlaps of multiple languages, cultures and economic structures. Certain populations cannot read Chinese signs so those graphics, in a way, disappear. I'm fascinated by how two cultures can share the same location but create two entirely different perceptual areas.

GDA: It's interesting that you speak about a density of cultures in an urban context. It's a very civic idea. How has this idea of civicness influenced your work?

PK: Our work for the visual campaign for Freshkills Park was entirely civic.

When presenting the identity, we always thought about the different audiences and constituencies. Local residents had been promised a park for a number of years and had never seen it materialize. As a site, Freshkills held a lot of negative connotations that it was hard for anyone to imagine something positive coming out of it. Our practice had to think about projecting forward: what might this park be in ten or 20 years? Who would the audiences be? How do we communicate these potentials to current residents as well as future park users? We had to think of ways to get people excited about the future.

GDA: I have to imagine the park's vast scale and time-frame made it a different type of

↑ **SCALED CONVERSATIONS**

1–2: *Designs for SALT (Istanbul). SALT hosts exhibitions, conferences and public programs; engages in interdisciplinary research projects; and sustains SALT Research, a library and archive of recent art, architecture, design, urbanism, and social and economic histories to make them available for research and public use.*

project. How did this idea of something emerging influence your work?

PK: This was a really important project for us because it shifted our way of thinking. We started working on Freshkills Park in 2006 and it was our largest commission until then. Prior to that we had designed a lot of exhibitions, books and websites, but this was Project Projects' first signage program. It was a different scale of signage, but also a different scale of time. The park was projected to take 30 or more years to complete, so we had to consider how to design a project that would not even exist for a half-century.

When built, Freshkills Park will be six times the size of Central Park and will have an incredible impact on New York's civic landscape. With this project, we had to shift our relationship to graphic design to think about things in the third person. Rather than developing a system that would look good only today, we had to reconsider the signage to think about how things make sense for the current as well as emerging context. When initially developing typographic systems, we had to put on a future lens. We didn't want our type choices to look outdated in three years. For example, the Vignellis' signage system for the [New York] Subway can go in and out of style, but something about it is timeless. It might look more or less contemporary at certain moments, but the signage is always iconic.

For our practice, it was the first time we had worked on a project of such permanence and it changed our sense of responsibility. We're making something not just for us, but for a city, for communities, that is going to impact people in a lot of ways that we can't always predict. We're not sure how people will use the park in the future so the signage had to address this uncertainty, too.

GDA: Most of your exhibitions are about displaying design ideas, not necessarily about exhibiting physical artifacts. How do you exhibit an idea?

PK: One of the problems that exists in exhibitions about graphic design or architecture is how to display the work. How do you represent the thing that exists in the world at a different scale?

In exhibiting architecture, you don't have quite the same relationship to objects as you do to, say, an exhibition about chairs or paintings. You don't have a set of artifacts that are invested with an aura and put them in connection with each other and create a narrative out of that. These types of exhibits start with a curatorial premise. We work with curators to not just present objects but to actually make other types of objects, make things for the space. The show we designed at the Canadian Centre for Architecture titled *Actions: What You Can Do with the City* featured 99 projects; all were small-scaled interventions and many didn't have a physical manifestation. So we designed books, pamphlets, posters and ephemeral objects to accompany the models and photos of the interventions.

GDA: How do you represent these design actions? How do you exhibit agency?

PK: I think that can be very difficult. Apart from architects, a lot of visitors aren't that engaged or invested in how you represent information. For example, we designed an exhibition with Ken Saylor called *Into the Open*. It was the New York Presentation of the 2008 Venice Biennale US Pavilion so we designed a completely new presentation. Curated by Bill Menking at the *Architect's Newspaper* and Aaron Beebe, it was a show about different grass roots architectural practices. The exhibit was located in the lobby of a new building at Parson's New School of Design. New fire code restrictions didn't allow students to hang posters in the lobby of the newly opened building.

↑ **SIGNING IDEAS**

3: *Signage program for Freshkills Park, 2007*

4: Into the Open, *Parson's New School of Design, New York*

5: Actions: What You Can Do with the City, *Canadian Centre for Architecture*

Students could come into the lobby and look at curated work, but students could not hang their own posters. So we conflated these ideas. The strategy for the exhibition display became about inviting student comments. We painted all of the walls and furniture in the space with green chalkboard paint, provided a shelf with chalk and invited students to write on the walls as they passed between their classes. As a result the exhibition took on an entirely different character. People used the exhibition so much it had to be cleaned and wiped down every week. The exhibit walls would be filled with people's writings. It was fascinating because the exhibition itself enacted something.

GDA: Do you seek ways to engage directly exhibition visitors? Do you typically invite visitors to interact with the work, touch the walls, change the exhibition?

PK: In different ways, we think about this. For *Graphic Design Now in Production*, the [Cooper–Hewitt, National Design Museum] presented an exhibition that originated at the Walker Arts Center. The exhibit was being held off-site on Governor's Island while their Manhattan museum space was being renovated. The temporary exhibition space on Governor's Island was a raw industrial space. It required expensive remediation simply to meet the Smithsonian's exhibition standards and was smaller than the exhibition space at the Walker. The Walker's space has beautiful white-walled galleries and, in that environment, graphic design work can be exhibited as an artwork.

Graphic design has a famous problem of having presence in that it requires context and site for it to have meaning. How do you represent an object such as book or poster, for example, that has a design relationship in the world: How do you take it out of the complex world and represent it in an isolated gallery space? I feel like this can be accomplished effectively through different display techniques. The natural history museum, for example, is purely objects and artifacts that in themselves may not have a lot of presence. But they are displayed in a way that reinvests them with an auratic quality. Exhibition design can have the difficult task of creating presence.

At the Governor's Island show, we expanded the exhibition to include a well-used hallway leading from the exhibit to the bathrooms. There are only two public

restrooms on the island, so anyone coming to the island for the day will inevitably find themselves, at some point, in this exhibition hallway. We turned a banal space into a small preview about the exhibition, using supergraphics and pieces from every section of the show. The hallway became a dense space. Anyone waiting in line for the restroom would interact with the exhibition.

We put some of the more interactive pieces in this hallway, too. Ideally someone sees something interesting in this bathroom hallway and they are compelled to walk into the museum exhibition—but even if they don't, they have been a part of the exhibition and engaged with it. And this is because the exhibition is located in a practical, infrastructural space, albeit an unconventional exhibition space.

GDA: What is your favorite part of the design process?

PK: For whatever reason, and I cannot tell you why, but the programming phase of a wayfinding project is really fun for me— it just clicks with the systematic part of my brain. Figuring out what information people need, which messages go where—that's an innate interest of mine.

When it comes to designing identities, I tend to approach them very theoretically. I also tend to think about curatorial and display with a more theoretical or meta objective. But with wayfinding, it's very direct. I just love to figure out which messages go where and I like to test these sequences. It's the conceptual and editorial part of my brain working in a practical way.

↑ **CONTEXT AND MEANING**

6–7: Graphic Design Now in Production, *Cooper–Hewitt, National Design Museum, Governor's Island, New York*

CREDITS

2x4 10, 12, 13, 14, 15, 205

ALL OF THE ABOVE 138, 139

STAN ALLEN ARCHITECTS 88, 89, 108, 109, 110, 111

KRISTY BALLIET 79

MATTHEW BANTON 31, 104, 105

NICHOLAS CASTILLO 172

BRANDON CLIFFORD 26, 28, 29, 31, 42

DUB STUDIOS 74, 75, 82, 83, 84, 85

AARON FRAZIER 80, 81

NICHOLAS FELTON 176, 177, 178, 179, 180, 181

FILSON AND ROHRBACHER 156, 157, 158, 159, 160, 161

BEN FLAUTE 23, 88, 89, 116, 124, 202, 203, 206, 208

BRIAN HAULTER 31

ELIJAH HUGE 78

IMPLEMENT 72, 73, 76, 77, 105, 129, 133

INTERBORO PARTNERS 96, 97, 98, 99, 100, 101

JANETTE KIM 136, 137, 138, 139, 140, 141

BRIAN KOEHLER 23, 34, 45, 104

LISL KOTHEIMER 26, 31, 35, 36, 44

KAYLE LANGFORD 173

SCOTT MCLEMORE 27

MICHAEL ODUM 24, 25, 62, 104, 106, 107

OPEN 194, 195, 196, 197, 198, 199

PROJECT PROJECTS 209, 210, 211, 212, 213, 214, 215

MATTHEW STORRIE 30, 35, 37, 43

THUMB 98, 99, 100, 101, 118, 119, 120, 121

URBAN LANDSCAPE LAB 136, 137, 140, 141

BENJAMIN VAN DYKE 66, 67, 68, 69

CHEYENNE VANDERVOORDE 129, 207, 209

WBOJ 50, 51, 52, 53

JESSIE WILCOX 30

INDEX

S

T

U

V

W

Y